INSTITUTE FOR PUBLIC POLICY RESEARCH

# Rationing Health Care

Stephen Harrison
and
David J Hunter

## IPPR'S Social Policy Programme

This report is the first of a new series from IPPR arising from the Institute's Social Policy Programme. The Programme encompasses health policy, local services and democracy, and family policy, as well as a major new study on media and communications. All this work takes a broad and long-term view of policy development. We seek to make connections, in intellectual and practical terms, between policy areas traditionally divided by departmental boundaries. And we aim to develop policies which are not only feasible in the short-term but also designed for maximum effect in the longer term. All the projects are concerned with issues of equity, the distribution of power, shared responsibility and economic viability. In the field of health, the current phase of the Social Policy Programme includes work on the development of rights and entitlement to health and health care, the process of planning for health gain, the future of primary care and the closer co-ordination of purchasing for health and local services.

The Social Policy Programme is supported by a wide range of charitable trusts and other organisations and companies, including the Paul Hamlyn Foundation, the Nuffield Foundation, the Leverhulme Trust, the Joseph Rowntree Foundation, the Baring Foundation, King Edward VII Hospital Fund for London, the Royal College of Nursing, Glaxo Pharmaceuticals UK, PPP, News International, BT and London Weekend Television. The programme is directed by Anna Coote, Hamlyn Fellow in Social Policy, and co-ordinated by Jane Franklin, Research Fellow.

# CONTENTS

*The authors are writing in a personal capacity*

## SUMMARY

### Introduction

The idea of rationing health care would seem to contradict the principles on which the National Health Service was founded: to provide 'a comprehensive health service designed to secure improvement in the physical and mental health of the people.' It is an unpopular idea with the public. It appears to conflict with medical ethics which hold that doctors should do their very best for every patient who comes their way. But the issue cannot be brushed aside. Rationing is unavoidable today and has in fact been practised within the NHS since its infancy.

Rationing is inevitable in any health care system where services are not charged directly to the patient, but are paid for indirectly through a third party (a scheme financed by the state or by private or social organisations). Consumers' demands will increase for services which they perceive to be free and good for them. Providers are inclined, for a variety of reasons, to encourage demand where there are no strong disincentives. And although the Beveridge Committee assumed that demand would be stemmed by better medical care improving the health of the population, nothing of the kind has happened. A return to direct payment-for-service is inconceivable, as it would leave all but the better-off without access to appropriate health care.

The fact that rationing is inevitable does not put it beyond the reach of policy-makers. Decisions must be made about ways and means of rationing, about who is involved in decision-making and about what criteria should guide rationing decisions.

## Ways and Means of Rationing

Resources can be allocated in different ways. For example, greater
or lesser priority can be given:

- to sectors of the population
- to forms of treatment
- to individual patients in allowing access to services
- to forms of treatment which might be given to individuals,
  once access is gained.

Patterns of decision-making do not necessarily progress in an
orderly fashion down this list. Different groups may be more or less
influential in decisions at each level. Furthermore, a range of
mechanisms for rationing may be employed:

### *Deterrence*

Introducing charges; making access inconvenient; putting up social
or psychological barriers.

### *Delay*

Queues and waiting list (may also deter or deflect).

### *Deflection*

Steering patients away from secondary to primary care; giving them
information about outcomes which may put them off demanding a
particular treatment.

### *Dilution*

Giving patients less treatment or cheaper drugs.

### *Denial*

Refusing to give certain forms of treatment to anyone, or to treat
certain individuals or groups.

In general, there is no legal redress for individuals who are subject to rationing of health care under current UK legislation.

## The Decision-Makers

There are six main groups who might be involved in rationing decisions. It is necessary to weigh up their respective strengths and weaknesses.

### The Medical Profession

Clearly this group is more highly esteemed by the public as a decision-maker in health care than any other group. However, there is little systematic knowledge about the basis of medical judgements. Doctors may implicitly deploy social criteria about who 'ought' to be treated. Doctor-led decisions are unlikely to be useful for macro-level rationing, since by culture and training, doctors are biased towards the individual, towards medical treatment in general rather than non-clinical preventative measures, and towards their own speciality.

### Health Authorities and their Managers

No not mue

Responsibility for rationing decisions is increasingly falling to this group. But they have no independent legitimacy as they are unelected and unaccountable, except to the Secretary of State.

### The Public

As service users and as taxpayers, the public has strong claims to a voice in rationing decisions. Health authorities have been ordered by government to consult the public. Some consultative exercises do little to explore in any depth the views of the public, or to make use of those views. Members of the public may be reluctant to take any responsibility for decisions, and may not have sufficient information on which to form opinions. Community Health Councils are supposed to represent the public's views. However, their legitimacy with the public may depend on their not being drawn into discussions about rationing.

## Central Government

Central government clearly has a legitimate role in health care rationing. However, in a large and complex democracy, links between the wishes of the electorate and the policies pursued by any government on this issue are inevitably weak. So far, central government has preferred to avoid explicit rationing.

## The Courts

The role of the courts could increase, especially if legislation were amended to provide explicit entitlements to health care, or to specify a basic health care package. Courts could then be involved in deciding whether new forms of treatment should be included in the package, or whether particular individuals needed any of the specified services. If courts were to decide on substantive matters of health care provision, this would take some power over resources away from government.

## Expert Groups

These can be broken down into different categories, with different interests in the rationing process. *Public health physicians* are interested in assessing health needs, for which they employ demographic, epidemiological and effectiveness data. *Health economists* use the same data, but are interested in how far health needs can be met within specific spending limits. Some *health statisticians* are more concerned with equitable allocation of expenditure at the macro level. *Philosophers* are increasingly intervening to question the criteria by which rationing decisions are made.

In general, members of the public prefer doctors to decide which forms of treatment should be given priority. Doctors and, more particularly, managers appear to favour a more pluralistic approach.

## Criteria for Rationing

So far, the debate about rationing criteria has been confused and unfocused. This is partly because the controversies inherent in most (if not all) of them have discouraged any move to render them explicit. Criteria which might guide decisions can be summed up as follows:

### *Effectiveness*

Few would disagree that it is sensible to favour interventions which have successful outcomes for the patient. But this can be hard to assess, since what is being considered is often not whether a 'cure' has occurred, but how the condition of an individual has been affected over a period. The effectiveness criterion may incorporate implicit value judgements which are hard to distinguish. It may also be difficult to determine which treatments are effective for which conditions. This may depend on the severity of the condition and the nature and circumstances of the individual, producing an almost infinite number of variables. Some of these 'treatment-condition pairings' may be considered inequitable.

### *Cost-effectiveness*

This is a way of ranking health care interventions by comparing the cost of one unit of good patient outcome produced by each intervention. This may be unproblematic at the micro level, when different treatments are considered for one diagnosis. But when the criterion is applied at the macro level, effectiveness can only be defined in the broadest of terms: the most common approach is set out below.

### *Cost-utility Analysis*

This measures cost-effectiveness by assessing the utility of an intervention to a notional patient in terms of the quality and length of life which can be expected as a result. Costs are calculated per Quality Adjusted Life Year (QALY), most often in order to produce league tables intended to help with decisions about whether a health care system should provide more or less of each item on a list of interventions. The approach has been heavily criticised. Evidence about outcomes is seldom clear or consistent. The utilitarian assumptions on which QALYs are based may be used to justify decisions which are widely considered immoral, such as neglect of the terminally ill. Controversial ethical and political judgements are concealed within an ostensibly technical formula.

### Non-instrumental Criteria

These allow for the possibility that measurably effective outcomes are not all that count. Public opinion favours heroic and costly attempts to save individuals, even if the chances of success are extremely slim. It can be argued that a publicly-funded service should respond to such preferences. The opportunity costs can be high: money spent on expensive rescue attempts may save more lives if diverted to more mundane uses. On the other hand, the unifying and civilising effects of simply doing one's best for one's fellow citizens should not be underestimated - and may even have a positive impact on the health of the population.

### 'Fair Goes'

In some circumstances, random selection could be seen as the fairest way of distributing scarce social goods. Versions of this criterion include selection by lottery, first-come-first-served, and going to the back of the queue for a second opportunity to receive treatment which did not work the first time.

### Need

Distribution according to need requires that need be distinguished from demand. Two basic human needs, survival/physical health and autonomy, can be understood as the essential preconditions for human action and interaction. But this interpretation of need provides only a partial criterion for rationing since what is required to meet need may cost more than government or society is willing to pay.

## Equity

This implies equal treatment for people with equal need and a consistent relationship between the extent of people's needs and the extent of their treatment. It is necessary to define what counts as 'treatment' and to decide which groups (since it is impracticable to compare individuals) are to be treated equally. Possible groups for comparison would include age cohorts, gender, ethnic groups, diagnostic categories and geographical areas. There are different measures of equity in health care: inputs, access and outcomes. Unequal distribution of inputs and access may be necessary to achieve outcomes that are more equally distributed between groups. The pursuit of equity in survival/physical health may conflict with the pursuit of equity of autonomy, eg. when people choose to damage their own health, although the problem may diminish if it is acknowledged that people need to sustain and improve their physical health and autonomy over time.

Two equity-based approaches to rationing, developed by the Dutch government and by the philosopher Ronald Dworkin, are described in more detail in the body of this report. The first assumes that all individuals should have an equal chance to function normally in society. Individuals, the medical professions and the community provide different perspectives on 'normal functioning', which must be weighed against each other. The following questions must then be asked: is care necessary and, if so, effective and, if so, efficient and, if so, not better left to individual responsibility.

The second introduces the 'prudent insurance principle'. This involves a thought experiment based on three hypotheses: wealth and income are more evenly distributed so that everyone has enough to live on; everyone has the same information about the costs and effectiveness of health care; and there is no basis on which to predict any individual's future health. In these circumstances, and in the absence of any existing state intervention in health care, for what eventualities and at what price would most fit young adults seek health insurance cover? The experiment is designed to help policy makers develop a basic health care package which would be available to all.

## *What are the Appropriate Criteria for Rationing?*

Health care is an essential component of citizenship, because it is one of the things that make it possible for individuals to participate in society. **Pursuit of equity** must therefore be the overriding objective. This involves:

●    equity of access to effective health care processes,

●    a healthy public policy in areas such as environment, transport and housing, and

●    equity of autonomy.

Policy should also take account of the need for:

●    maintaining a sense of social solidarity;

●    fair procedures to legitimise decisions;

●    efficient management to minimise opportunity costs;

●    co-ordination of health services with other policy sectors which impact upon health.

## Options for Public Policy

The aim is to create favourable conditions for implementing the ideas outlined above. Two scenarios are offered as a way of testing possibilities.

### *Scenario I: Local Democratic Representation*

Local government authorities would become the purchasers of health care from the present providers. This could offer:

- democratic legitimacy for health care planning and rationing,

- integrated planning and purchasing for health and social care,

- health treatment and care brought within a policy arena which includes other important determinants of health.

Opponents of the idea have claimed that local government is not really democratic at all. Local decision-making would undermine the national character of the NHS, by introducing diverse ways of defining and meeting need. It could lead to competition between localities, fiscal migration, and new and compounded patterns of inequality. Against this it can be argued that central government is hardly more democratic than local government. In general, a new model of local governance would be required. Local diversity should operate within certain statutory constraints: first, to ensure that purely social judgements were not used to establish entitlements and, second, to impose a general duty to pursue equity of outcome.

### Scenario II: National Health Care Rights

National legislation would establish a set of explicit health care rights, based on equity of access to an agreed health care package. If district health authorities had the duty to enforce these rights, funding could be based upon an actuarial assessment of local needs and costs, with a central contingency fund to meet excess demands. To accommodate the need for tight control over the central budget, statutory rights would cover a basic minimum and DHAs would have some financial headroom to provide services not covered by statute. The complex job of defining statutory entitlements could be carried out by a Standing Commission, which would take account of expert knowledge as well as public (though not populist) opinion, and keep technological and other changes under review.

### Assessing the Options

In weighing up the options, it will be useful to consider the following questions:

● *Centralisation*

  How far can decisions be devolved to localities? How far should the centre retain control, and over what issues?

● *Integration*

  How far should planning and purchasing for health care be integrated with other public services?

● *Explicitness*

  How far should criteria for rationing and the rationing process itself be open and explicit?

● *Physical health care or more?*

  How far should planning and rationing be concerned with a wide range of objectives, including autonomy and holistic notions of health?

● *Organisational change*

  To what extent is radical organisational change desirable?

The two scenarios can be considered separately or in combination, with the first operating within a framework defined by the second. All these matters need further exploration, to understand how the different options might work in practice. This paper attempts to map out the territory for policy makers, and so help to build a robust policy towards rationing health care.

# INTRODUCTION

The notion that health care is, and must be, rationed is still a controversial one. On the political right, it is associated with a lack of freedom and the bogey of 'state planning'. On the political left, it may be seen solely as a consequence of Tory underfunding of the National Health Service (NHS). As Rudolf Klein says: 'The word 'rationing' is invoked in order to make to flesh creep, not to prompt argument about how best to deal with the inescapable.' (Klein, 1992a, p.2). Indeed, rationing may well seem to be a denial of the very principles upon which the NHS was founded: the provision of a *comprehensive* health service designed to secure improvement in the physical and mental health of the people...' (National Health Service Act, 1946, S1(1), emphasis added.)

Even outside the realm of party politics, the notion of rationing remains an uncomfortable one. 'You can't put a price on a life', one wishes to say. Politicians, of course, are acutely aware of this public perspective; in a context where the NHS is the most popular sector of the UK welfare state and consistently receives high levels of overall positive responses in opinion polls (Taylor-Gooby, 1985; Judge and Solomon, 1993), talk of health care rationing looks like a vote-loser. Seventy per cent of respondents to a 1991 opinion poll replied negatively to the question 'Should the government restrict some non-essential treatments available on the NHS?' (Davies, 1991). No wonder that, following the lead set by the Labour government's 1976 *Priorities* document (DHSS, 1976), the unpronounceable 'prioritisation' has been preferred to the brutal R-word. (For a further discussion, see Jonsen 1992.)

Rationing may even seem to conflict with medical professional ethics, whose approach is based on an individualism which fails to consider resource allocation at the social level (McGuire, 1986, p.1167-8). As one consultant surgeon wrote: 'It is one thing to tell relatives that, on clinical grounds a problem is inoperable, but who would suggest it's inoperable on financial grounds? Certainly no caring clinician would do this - maybe an administrator would!' (Magell, 1985, p.3). The insinuation in the second sentence demonstrates the powerful negative symbolism of rationing - deployed in this case to attack NHS management.

Yet in spite of a tacit pretence that rationing does not occur, or is merely a product of policies one opposes, the topic is increasingly discussed by policy commentators. There have been special issues of *Health Management Quarterly* (Vol. XIV, No. 2, 1992), *Health Care Analysis*, (Vol. 1, No. 1, 1993) and *Critical Public Health* (Vol. 4, No. 1, 1993) devoted to the topic, a survey conducted for the *British Medical Journal* (13 March 1993), and a computer simulation-based exercise for NHS purchasing authorities (Griffith and McMahon, 1992). Many other journals have carried single articles on the topic (see, for instance, Smith, 1992; Culyer, 1992). Not surprisingly, the doctors' professional journal and its managerial equivalents, have carried numerous pieces (see, for instance, Heginbotham, 1992; Klein, 1993; Redmayne and Klein, 1993; Lyall, 1993a) and the National Association of Health Authorities and Trusts has published two substantial monographs (Mooney *et al*, 1992; Hunter, 1993a). Interest in the topic is neither confined to the UK (we refer to the 'Oregon formula' and debate in the Netherlands below) nor to health (Stewart, 1990).

The purpose of this paper is to contribute to the present debate in two ways. First, there is a 'ground-clearing' exercise, since we believe that much of the debate so far has been narrow and confused. Second, we provide some tentative policy options: it seems to us that the debate is a difficult one for politicians to handle, partly because of the negative connotations we have described, and partly because of a reluctance to separate rationing from debates about levels of public spending.

We begin by arguing that rationing health care *is unavoidable*. In order to establish this, we start from what may be regarded as first principles in the establishment of a health service, and show that both the necessity for rationing and methods of so doing are in effect built into it. Next, we identify three related aspects of rationing where policy choices *do* exist: there are choices about *who* rations, *what mechanisms* are employed, and *what criteria* are employed. We consider a range of possibilities and offer some comment on current UK practice and trends. Finally, we identify two broad policy options which merit closer examination.

We recognise that the matters with which we are concerned cannot, and should not, be depoliticised, however alluring the prospect of contemporary technical 'fixes' such as QALYs (see below). As one famous doctor-turned-politician commented around a century ago: 'Medicine is a social science and politics nothing else but medicine on a large scale.' (Virchow, 1887).

## WHY IS RATIONING INEVITABLE?

To address this question, we must return to first principles: what is
a health service, and for what purposes does it ostensibly exist? A
hypothetical situation in which no health service exists is illustrated
in Figure 1.

**Figure 1: Out-of-Pocket Payment for Health Care**

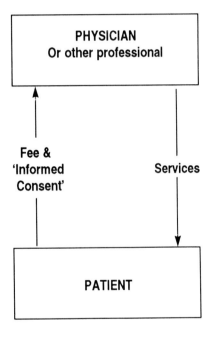

*Source*: Harrison S (1988) *Managing the NHS: Shifting the Frontier?*, London,
Chapman and Hall, p.4.

## Out of Pocket Payment

In these circumstances, the doctor (or midwife, or dentist, etc.) derives his or her income from fees. There may well be elements of charitable behaviour, but there are obvious limits: were a professional to subsidise the poor too heavily, fees for other patients would rise, leading to their migration to the care of less charitable professionals. Hence, in general, so long as the patient can and will pay, and gives consent to treatment, health services will be provided. From some perspectives, such a mode of organising health care - which we call *'out of pocket payment'* has its attractions: it is relatively simple to organise and largely avoids the direct involvement of government. Few countries in the world now rely wholly or mainly upon this model for the organisation of their health care services. However, it continues to provide the ideology for professional (especially medical) ethics in which there is a fiction that a relationship exists which involves only the professional and the patient, with the former free from the influence of any third party. The BMA puts it thus:

> Within the [NHS] resources are finite and this may restrict the freedom of the doctor to advise his [sic] patient .... [and thus] infringes the *ordinary* relationship between patient and doctor .... The doctor has a general duty to advise on equitable allocation and efficient utilisation [but this] is subordinate to his professional duty to the individual who seeks his clinical advice (British Medical Association, 1980, p.35, emphasis added).

Out-of-pocket payment for health care is obviously hard on those who cannot afford to pay directly. It is worth noting that, at present day costs of medical care, it would not only be the very poorest members of society who would be unable to afford it. The answer to this problem, adopted in some form or other in most countries in the world, is a system of *'third party payment'* for health care. This is illustrated in Figure 2 overleaf.

## Figure 2: Third Party Payment for Health Care

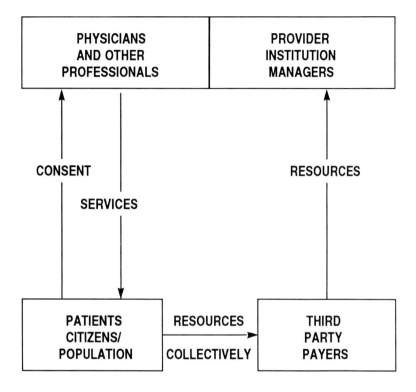

Source: Adapted from Harrison S (1988) *Managing the NHS*, London, Chapman and Hall, 1988.

## Third Party Payment

The purpose of such systems (of which the UK NHS is one specific example) is to divorce receipt of health services, which persons receive *qua* patient, from payment for services, which they make *qua* members of a population group. (We return to this below.) Financial resources are collected by 'third party payers' and routed directly to hospitals and other providers of care.

The identity of the parties, and the resource collection arrangements, vary from country to country. The 'population' may literally be all citizens/residents, as in the UK, and the resource collection may (again, as in the UK) be *via* the general taxation system, so that the third party payer is the central government. But many other arrangements are found. Social insurance systems may have different arrangements for different sub-populations within a country (perhaps varying by region and/or occupation and/or industry in which employed), so that members' contributions may be made to one of several 'sickness funds' or by a central insurance fund agency. Even private health insurance systems function on the same basis; there are populations of insured persons (in different schemes and/or with different insurance companies) who pay premia; the insurance companies act as the third party payers. (For a general review of health care financing mechanisms, see Culyer *et al*, 1988.)

Despite the differences, the basic policy intention in all the above cases is the same, that is to socialise to some extent the financial consequences of ill-health. This does not, of course, mean that all types of third party payment system are equally successful in this socialisation effort. Other things being equal, compulsory tax-financed systems, such as the UK's, are most successful in this respect since they can ensure (as far as the particular tax system allows) that all citizens contribute in relation to their ability to pay and are entitled to receive services in relation to their 'need'. There may, however, be practical problems on both supply and demand sides - for example, tax evasion or avoidance, and the fact that ability to articulate health care needs may not be distributed evenly between social classes.

The concept of 'need' is itself problematic. Those who demand care and those who provide it may have different and even conflicting views of the would-be patient's needs. In present practice, therefore, what is called 'need' is an amalgam of demands by citizens and demands by professional health care providers, especially, though not exclusively, doctors. (Of course, there are other approaches to the question of need; we discuss these below.) Given such circumstances, third party payment systems for health care institutionalise two phenomena which together necessitate the rationing of health services.

### Consumer Moral Hazard

One may be termed *consumer moral hazard* (Arrow, 1963): that is, the tendency for an individual entitled to free services to reason along the lines that 'a modest additional demand on my part will not significantly affect total spending and will not therefore affect my taxes or health insurance premium'. Of course, if many individuals behave in this way, the conclusion will be mistaken. The point is that demand will tend to exceed supply where there is no *apparent* cost, and, as a result, third party payment systems are unlikely to be able to meet all demands. It should be noted, however, that the argument is not that demand is infinite, but only that it is infinite for something which is free to those who demand it, and *believed* by them to do them good. Some people, for example those who prefer 'alternative' health therapies, do not believe that certain kinds of medical care do one good. Others, for instance self carers, believe that their demands are not met by the NHS.

Three common objections to the necessity for rationing have less force than is sometimes supposed. First, it is not sufficient merely to observe, as did one prominent Labour politician, (*The Guardian*, 18 May 1992, p.20) that in fact a good deal of health care is ineffective or, at best, unproven. 'Goodness' is in the eye of the demander. So long as people believe that any aspect of health care is, or might be, effective, they will continue to demand it. As we shall see, persuading people to change this belief is, in principle, one approach to rationing.

Second, it does not help to point out that demand for certain *specific* health care interventions is finite, that, for instance, no-one has more than one appendix, or uterus, to be surgically removed. In other words, arguments that all demands for specific interventions can be met (see, for instance, Williams and Frankel, 1993, p.15) cannot be extended towards the conclusion that *total* demand is finite. Indeed, as Klein (1989, 1992) has pointed out, it can be misleading to think of demand in terms primarily of high technology or acute intervention. Rather, future demand is likely to be much more related to *care*, including social care:

Even if the limitations of medical technology in curing disease and disability are now becoming apparent, there are no such limitations on the scope of health services for providing care for those who cannot be cured. Even if policies of prevention and social engineering were to be successfully introduced, their very success in extending life expectancy would create new demands for alleviating the chronic degenerative diseases of old age. In short, no policy can ensure that people will drop dead painlessly at the age of 80, not having troubled the health services previously (Klein, 1989, p.182).

Finally, the empirical observation that no country at present spends more than about fourteen per cent of its gross domestic product on health care does not help. The general trend is upwards, influenced both by the continuing development of medical technology (despite Klein's comments), and the increasingly ageing populations of many countries (OECD, 1987).

### Supplier-Induced Demand

The second problematic phenomenon for third-party payment systems is *supplier-induced demand*, sometimes known as provider moral hazard. This reflects the fact that it is difficult for consumers to make well-informed choices about their doctors or other suppliers of health care, or about the treatments that they desire (Harris, 1993, p.30). This is not just the result of technical complexity. The personal computer is a technically complex product, and so is the motor car, but specialist interest magazines or consumer publications such as *Which?*, all reporting on features such as reliability, maintenance costs, and prices, allow consumers to make fairly well-informed choices, provided that they are prepared to put in a modicum of effort. Even though it has been proposed that hospitals should publish, for instance, their surgical mortality rates and 'league tables' of comparative information about NHS performance for the use of the general public (NHSME, 1993), comparable consumer information is rarely available in respect of health. *Even if it were*, however, it is far from clear that it would be usable in the same way as (say) *Which?* fuel consumption data, since humans are rather less standardised than motor cars. It is easy to understand what '35 miles per gallon' means to us as individuals; it less easy to be sure of the implications of the fact that the Infirmary's perioperative mortality rate is n percent, or that vasectomy seems to result in a 66 percent (rising to 85 percent after 22 years) elevated risk of cancer of the prostate (Giovannucci *et al*, 1993).

On the whole, people do not behave as 'customers' of health care professionals and provider institutions, but as *clients*:

> The customer is always right; he [sic] can choose, criticise, and reject. The client on the other hand, gives up these privileges and accepts the superior judgement of the professional (Gower Davies, 1972, p.220).

'It hurts here', we say to the doctor, implying 'Please help'. This is another reason why, as we have already noted, 'need' for health care is demand mediated by professionals acting on behalf of their patients; patients do not, in general, demand operations, pathology tests, or anti-depressants. Rather, doctors do. In situations where doctors and/or the institutions in which they work are reimbursed on a fee-for-service basis and where there are no total expenditure caps, there is therefore a strong incentive to multiply services to the patient. But even where this is not so (as in the UK at present), in a third party payment system where the provider does not have to fear bad debts, he or she has little disincentive to do everything that might help every patient, unless prevented from so doing by resource restrictions.

The brutal consequences of the combination of consumer and provider moral hazard in a system of third party payment such as the NHS necessarily means that *health care will be rationed*: that is, not everyone will receive all of the care that either they or their professional carers would like. We are therefore using the term 'ration' in a broad sense; we do not mean to imply that health care must necessarily be rationed in the *calculated* way in which, say, foodstuffs may be rationed in wartime. (For a discussion, see Baker,

1992.) Other terms might be substituted ('demand curtailment'?), but in any event it will not be helpful to take refuge from the issues of substance in a verbal debate.

## The Beveridge fallacy

The debate about rationing may be a new feature on the political and professional landscape, but clearly the phenomenon of rationing is not new to the NHS. The assumptions of Beveridge Committee in 1942 provide a stark contrast:

> It is a logical corollary to the payment of high benefits in disability that determined efforts should be made by the state to reduce the number of cases for which benefit is needed (Committee on Social Insurance and Allied Services, 1942, para 426).

> [The cost of] further development of the service would be offset by the fall in demand which would take place once the original backlog of need had been wiped out, and the population became healthier as a result of better medical care .... (Watkin, 1978, p.28).

This mistaken assumption, though it was perhaps not evident as such until the NHS had been in existence for several years (see, for instance, Roberts, 1952), is commonly referred to as the 'Beveridge fallacy'.

That rationing is inevitable does not put the matter beyond the scope of politics and policy-making. In particular, there are three related areas of political choice.

- Who makes rationing decisions?
- By what mechanisms are these implemented?
- By what criteria are rationing decisions made?

Our next section deals with the first two; the following section deals with the third. In both these sections, we undertake a broad review of the possibilities that exist, and of current and past practices.

## WHO RATIONS, AND HOW?

As long ago as 1979, at Edinburgh University, a seminar series on the ethics of resource allocation in health care identified four broad competing views about health care rationing. (Boyd *et al*, 1979) These are summarised in Box 1 opposite.

This work is notable, both because of its foresightedness and because it reminds us that a wider range of views exists than is commonly reported. In fact, the 'clinical argument', implicitly dominant in the UK since (at least) the inception of the NHS, appears to be losing ground to the more explicit 'administrative argument', perhaps with a genuflection in the direction of the 'epidemiological/ecological argument' (*The Health of the Nation*: Department of Health *et al* 1992 - for instance). As we shall see, the purchaser/provider split is an important mechanism for this shift. The fourth, 'egalitarian argument' is rarely heard in mainstream policy-making discussions.

The Edinburgh analysis fails, however, to observe that there are at least four different dimensions to rationing.

> Firstly, there are decisions about the allocation of resources to broad sectors or client groups. Secondly, there are decisions about the allocation of resources to specific forms of treatment (particularly those which require investment in new facilities) within those broad sectors or groups. Thirdly, there are decisions about how to prioritise access to treatment between different patients. Fourthly, there are decisions about how much to invest in individual patients - by way of diagnostic procedures and so on - once access has been achieved (Klein, 1992b, p.1458).

However, there are two problems with this form of analysis. Firstly, there is an implication that the four dimensions are of decreasing generality, that is that the decision making progresses from the first to the fourth, in that order. But this is not *necessarily* the case, even

# Box 1
# The Ethics of Resource Allocation in Health Care - Four Views

*Ecological/Epidemiological Arguments:*

The Earth is a limited resource, health is primarily endangered by:

● environmental factors which unbalance its equilibrium with its inhabitants;
● behavioural factors.

Health policy should therefore concentrate on research into causes of ill-health, and upon attempts to change unhealthy behaviour.

*Clinical Argument:*

1. Habits are difficult to change, and the new ones could turn out to be unhealthy.
2. Survival is people's first priority, recovery from acute illness their second.
3. Human lives are of equal value: rationing should be on 'first-come, first-served' basis.

*Administrative Argument:*

1. Fair rationing requires more information about:
   (a) population/patient needs and (b) effectiveness of treatment.
2. Rational systems can be constructed to put the above criteria into operation.

*Egalitarian Argument:*

1. Higher social classes benefit disproportionately both from curative and preventive services.
2. Professionals mystify and monopolise knowledge, and secure for themselves privileged conditions of work.
3. Health policy should concentrate on redressing inequalities, e.g. housing, cash benefits.

*Source*: (summarised from) Boyd K M, *et al* (Eds) (1979) *The Ethics of Resource Allocation in Health Care*: Edinburgh, Edinburgh University

though it is what tends to happen in the UK. For instance, there is no reason why the decision makers could not start by expressing their overarching priorities in terms of treatments (Klein's second dimension), rather than in terms of groups such as the elderly, or children (Klein's first dimension). Indeed, client groups do not have to be identified at all. Perhaps the only robust distinction is between the determination of entitlement on priority for classes of prospective patient (the macro level), and the placing of individual patients within those classes (the micro level).

The second problem is related to the first. There is an obvious temptation to see Klein's first two dimensions (as do Klein himself, and Hoffenberg, 1992) as the territory of policy-makers, perhaps after wide consultation, and the remaining ones as that of doctors. This may be in line with current UK practice, but is it the only possible approach? In fact, it is not. For example, as Heginbotham (1992, p.497) has pointed out, health insurance companies in the United States are currently attempting, through a combination of prospective and current case review, to control Klein's third and fourth dimensions. It does not, however, follow that it is equally practicable to allocate first and second dimension decisions to doctors. Given the individualistic ethical basis of medicine (see above) and the highly specialised basis of much medical training, it is probably unrealistic to expect doctors not to be strongly biased in favour of their own specialism (McGuire, 1986, p.1172).

It is thus clear that the 'who' and 'how' of rationing are closely related to each other. In order to explore the possibilities, we begin by examining the various rationing *mechanisms* which exist, before going on to consider the implications of these for the identity of the decision makers. It should be remembered that at this stage we are describing mechanisms rather than making judgements about them.

## Mechanisms for Rationing

Mechanisms for rationing health care can conveniently be classified under five headings, as follows: (cf. Hunter, 1993a; Parker, 1975)

## Deterrence

Demands for health care can be obstructed. *Co-payments* are the most obvious way of doing this. They may come in several forms, including fixed charges for services (as with UK prescriptions, for instance), 'coinsurance' of a fixed percentage of charges (as with UK general dental procedures), and 'deductibles' or 'excesses' which (as in UK motor car insurance) consist of a fixed deduction from third party reimbursement. Small charges are least likely to deter large numbers, although of course the poorest people are most likely to be deterred by any level of charges. Since the poorest are often those with the greatest health care needs, charges will be inequitable (see below) as a means of rationing unless they are closely related to individuals' incomes.

Other means of deterrence include inconvenient location of services, so as to provide effective physical barriers. There is a good deal of evidence to suggest that proximity to hospitals explains a good deal of the small area variation in health service utilisation (Clarke *et al*, 1993), and the story of the American health maintenance organisation which required would-be subscribers to register in person on the seventh floor of an office block with no lift may or may not be apocryphal. It is also possible to erect psychological and social barriers to access: highly bureaucratic or other user-unfriendly procedures function in this way.

## Delay

Both the physical queues found in some countries and the system of hospital waiting lists familiar in the UK fall into the category of delay, since they function as a kind of holding area to buffer excess demand. (There is also evidence, entirely ignored by the UK government's Waiting List Initiative, that waiting times also have a *deterrent* effect. See, for instance, Goldacre *et al* 1987.) According to Higgins and Ruddle (1991, p.18) the UK government made a conscious choice of waiting lists in preference to widespread charges during the 1950s when the 'Beveridge fallacy' first became apparent. Waiting lists may also have a *deflection* effect (see below) in that the desire to circumvent them is a major factor in sustaining the UK private health care sector (Calnan *et al* 1993, pp.60-5).

## Deflection

In the UK context, the most important mechanism for the deflection of health care demand into different channels is the general medical practitioner (GP). Except in emergencies, a person cannot gain direct access to hospitals or other secondary care services without referral by a GP, who acts as a 'gatekeeper'. Thus GPs often deflect demand from secondary health care, into the continuation of primary care treatment by themselves, or occasionally by referral to another agency, such as social services.

Another means of deflection, which attracts increasing interest, is to provide patients with more information. As one NHS manager put it:

> If we give people more information about outcomes and side-effects, it is possible that more people will choose not to go ahead with particular operations and treatments (F Winkler, quoted in Meek, 1992, p.17).

One Regional Health Authority has recently developed a video which explores the consequences of, and alternatives to, prostatectomy (Lyall, 1993b). This approach has also been employed in the United States, where initial research has shown that when candidates for treatment are shown the video they are less likely to decide to have the operation. (Wennberg, 1990)

## Dilution

Responses to health care demand can be diluted by a reduction of quality. For example, cheaper prostheses or drugs might be used in place of the best. In practice, of course, it is not always easy to tell the difference between dilution which actually lowers quality, and improvements in efficiency which cut out waste. Continued disputes over the desirability of generic prescribing or the development of expensive new drugs with contested benefits (see, for example, the review by Freemantle *et al*, 1993 of anti-depressant drugs) illustrate the scope for disagreement.

A less obvious, but more important, means of dilution is the exercise of 'clinical freedom': this is the doctrine that a fully-qualified clinical doctor has the freedom to make treatment decisions on behalf of his or her patient, with the patient's consent, but without the involvement of any hierarchical superior. (For a fuller discussion, see Harrison, 1988, chap.2; Harrison *et al*, 1984.) Throughout the history of the NHS, UK governments have been much attached to the notion. Box 2 contains a selection of official statements on the topic, made by governments of both main persuasions, between 1944 and 1979.

---

### Box 2
### UK Governments and Clinical Freedom

'Whatever the organisation, the doctors taking part must remain free to direct their clinical knowledge and personal skill for the benefit of the patients in the way in which they feel to be best' (White Paper *A National Health Service*, Ministry of Health, 1944, p.26).

'The Service should provide full clinical freedom to the doctors working in it' (Crossman Green Paper *The Future Structure of the National Health Service*, DHSS, 1970, p.1).

The organisational changes will not affect the ... relationship between individual patients and individual professional workers ... [who] ... will retain their clinical freedom ... to do as they think best for their patients' (Joseph White Paper, *National Health Service Reorganisation: England*, DHSS, 1972a, pvii).

'Success ... depends primarily on the people in the health care professions who prevent, diagnose and treat disease. Management plays only a subsidiary part ...' ('Grey Book', *Management Arrangements for the Reorganised National Health Service*, DHSS, 1972b, p.9).

'It is doctors, dentists and nurses and their colleagues in the other health professions who provide the care and cure of patients ... It is the purpose of management to support them in giving that service' (*Patients First*, DHSS and Welsh Office, 1979, pp.1-2).

---

This adherence to clinical freedom is not surprising, for it has the effect of making rationing decisions politically invisible (Harrison, 1988, p.125; Hunter, 1993a, p.27). In Box 3, two American observers of the British NHS, describe the process applied to particularly dramatic (ultimately life or death) circumstances.

---

**Box 3**
**Clinical Freedom as a Rationing Mechanism**

By various means, physicians ... try to make the denial of care seem routine or optimal. Confronted by a person older than the prevailing unofficial age of cut-off for dialysis, the British GP tells the victim of chronic renal failure or his [sic] family that nothing can be done except to make the patient as comfortable as possible in the time remaining. The British nephrologist tells the family of a patient who is difficult to handle that dialysis would be painful and burdensome and that the patient would be more comfortable without it (H J Aaron and W B Schwartz, *The Painful Prescription*: Washington D.C., The Brookings Institution, 1984, p.101).

---

Generalising their observations, which of course do not apply only in extremes, the same authors comment:

> The British physician often seems to adjust his [sic] indications for treatment to bring into balance the demand for care and the resources available to provide it. This kind of rationalisation preserves as much as possible the feeling that all care of value is being provided. Most patients in Britain appear willing to accept their doctor's word if he says that no further treatment of a particular disease is warranted (Aaron and Schwartz, 1984, p.111).

In other words, not only is the illusion of a comprehensive and unlimited health service maintained, but politicians and others are spared unpleasant and politically embarrassing decisions about rationing. It is easy to see how difficult it would be for any Secretary of State for Health to announce in the House of Commons that no-one over the age of n years would in future receive renal dialysis. (A similar problem has arisen in *social* care: see *The Guardian*, 28 December 1992, p.2, where it was reported that local authorities had been asked not to identify needs which they could not meet.)

This approach to rationing, however, requires the co-operation of the medical profession (Hoffenberg, 1987, p.13), and there are increasing signs that this is no longer so readily available; the British Medical Association, for instance, at its 1992 conference called on the government to make explicit decisions. In any case, the growth of managerialism in the NHS has made clinical autonomy less viable as a policy option (Harrison and Pollitt, 1994, ch.6).

*Denial*

Although Aaron and Schwartz (above) use the term 'denial', most exercises of clinical freedom are examples of dilution, in that *some* form of treatment is provided. But the possibility of complete denial of treatment has arrived on the policy agenda with the creation of the 'purchaser/provider split' in the NHS. Indeed one of the main rationales for making the split is to facilitate the process of identifying *and prioritising* health care needs in a population (Harrison, 1991, p.630). Authorities' early denial decisions, and discussion abut them, have centred on *in vitro* fertilisation ('test tube babies') (Harrison and Wistow, 1992; Redmayne and Klein, 1993; Ham, 1993), though other procedures, especially plastic surgery to remove tattoos, have also been discussed as candidates. It is worth pointing out that, expensive as some of these procedures may be, *total* expenditure on them is a very small proportion of health expenditure. From a central government point of view, political embarrassment about rationing may be diffused if decisions to deny some forms of treatment are taken locally. As the present Secretary of State for Health put it:

> [central government] is *not* the appropriate level at which
> to take decisions on clinical priority. Those decisions
> should be taken locally. They must involve managers,
> consultants, GPs, nurses and the public (Bottomley, 1993,
> p.6, emphasis original).

In contrast, the Labour Party has argued that these local decision-
makers at least require guidance:

> The Conservatives have failed to offer help and guidance
> to doctors in tackling the choices to be made every day in
> allocating scarce resources. Labour is concerned that any
> prioritising process should be fair and accountable. We
> recognise that there are difficult decisions to be made and
> it would be unacceptable for government to interfere in
> the clinical judgement of those having to make such
> decisions. However, we have a duty to provide support
> and guidance and to acknowledge the pressures which
> exist (Labour Party, 1994, p.31).

In practice, however, few such explicit decisions have *yet* been
taken locally. Purchasing authorities have so far preferred either to
urge government to publish guidelines or to leave matters largely in
the hands of the doctors employed by provider institutions (Harrison
and Wistow, 1992; Salter, 1993; Redmayne *et al*, 1993). One
technique for 'fudging' matters in this way is set out in Box 4
opposite.

More recent research suggests that health authorities would like to
develop guidelines to indicate which patients are likely to benefit
from particular treatments. (Ham, 1993, p.435).

### Summary of Mechanisms

These, then, are five basic approaches to the mechanics of rationing.
It should be noted that British courts, unlike those in the United
States (Ferguson, *et al*, 1993), have not as yet challenged the
rationing process (Baker, 1992, p.214) when asked to rule on

---

**Box 4**
**Rationing by NHS Purchasing Authorities:**
**Just How Explicit?**

A third development was the consideration being given to the level of funding for 'low priority treatments'. One authority was faced with a provider unit developing expensive procedures in the expectation that they would be purchased by the DHA. However, the latter had already announced its decision not to purchase one of them (IVF, largely on grounds of its perceived ineffectiveness). In addition, the DHA's officers were considering recommending that the authority cut or abandon a number of other services (for example, rhinoplasty and breast surgery for cosmetic purposes, all removals of tattoos and warts, and varicose vein surgery). It was possible the authority would decide that such procedures should not be available at all. Other authorities did not envisage blanket refusals to provide such treatments but anticipated agreeing to purchase only very limited numbers each year in specified circumstances (for example, tattoo removal in cases of psychological distress). In all cases, the lists of 'low priority' treatments had been drawn up in consultation with public health physicians, *though it was largely expected that it would be the hospital consultants (i.e. the providers) who would act as the 'gatekeeper' of access.*

*Source*: S Harrison & G Wistow, 'The Purchaser/Provider Split in English Health Care: Towards Explicit Rationing?', *Policy and Politics*, Vol. 20, No. 2, 1992, emphasis added.

---

entitlement to treatment. The current legal doctrine seems to be that the Secretary of State's duty (originally established in the National Health Service Act of 1946) to provide a 'comprehensive health service' leaves considerable discretion; attempts by would-be patients to use the law against the government have failed (Dimond, 1993, p.27; McHale and Hughes, 1993, p.23).

We now proceed to the related question of *who* makes rationing decisions.

## The Decision Makers

There are five main groups who are candidates for this role: the medical profession, health authorities and their managers, the public, the government, and the courts.

### *The Medical Profession*

The medical professions, especially clinical doctors, clearly possess a great deal of legitimacy. Public opinion polls of occupational esteem frequently place doctors among the groups with 'the highest standards of ethics and honesty' or 'most likely to tell the truth' (Harrison, 1988, pp.88-9). Indeed, it is precisely this esteem which supports the process of rationing by clinical autonomy which we have described. But there are at least three difficulties with the assumption that rationing decisions can be left to doctors as a matter of future policy. The first is that we have very little systematic knowledge about the basis of medical judgements. Certainly, they are often based on a loose belief about what is good for the patient, but we also know that these beliefs are often misplaced (Freemantle *et al*, 1993b) and anyway (as we discuss in the next Section) it is not *self evident* that this is the appropriate criterion. Moreover, clinicians often base their treatment decisions on implicit social judgements (Pollock, 1993, p.21), a matter to which we shall return.

A second difficulty with doctor-led rationing is that it is unlikely to be of much use at the macro level, since by both culture and training doctors are biassed to the individual, to medical treatment in general (rather than towards, say, prevention or environmental policies), and to their own specialty.

The third difficulty is, of course, that times change. There appears to be a greater readiness on the part of the public to criticise, though not yet necessarily challenge, the medical profession, though it is hard to provide systematic evidence for such a trend. Nor is it clear that doctors themselves wish to carry on in this way. Finally, it may be that doctors' legitimacy as rationers can only be sustained while rationing is not seen to happen. The kind of discussion to which this paper contributes implies, however, that we have lost our innocence in this respect.

## Health Authorities and their Managers

Rationing decisions are increasingly falling upon health authorities, especially since the introduction of the purchaser/provider split to the NHS. As we have noted, one Secretary of State for Health has identified the health authority as the appropriate locus for such decisions, within a framework of wide consultation. However, NHS managers (including non-executive directors of health authorities) have no *independent* legitimacy as decision makers. Legally, they are agents of the Secretary of State and changes to the membership of health authorities which followed the *Working for Patients* 'reforms' mean that there is no longer automatic representation of elected local government (Coote, 1993, p.38). Such bodies are not sociologically representative of their public: women, ethnic minorities and lower social classes are heavily under-represented (see, for instance, Ashburner and Cairncross, 1993, pp.366-70). The democratic legitimacy of managers as rationing agents can only, therefore, derive from elsewhere - either from central government itself, or from managers' own attempts to consult their local communities. At least some NHS managers find this an uncomfortable position. David Knowles, President of the Institute of Health Services Managers, told the IHSM Annual Conference in June 1993 that in his view local government should take over the purchasing function from health authorities (*Health Service Journal*, 1993, p.13). This, he said, would overcome the 'lack of legitimacy' managers feel in making decisions on behalf of the community. The view is shared by others, notably the local government analyst, John Stewart, who is critical of the 'new magistracy' in British public life which controls large areas of policy but which owes its allegiance to central government not the local communities it serves (Stewart, 1993).

## Public Consultation

There is a wide spectrum of health authority attitudes towards *public consultation* (Harrison and Wistow, 1992, p.128). Some District Health Authorities are employing large-scale consultation exercises (Meek, 1992, p.16) though a number of commentators have dismissed them as something of a mockery, on the grounds that the enquiry can be structured so as to produce the results desired by managers (Meek, 1992; Coote, 1993, p.39; Pollock, 1992, p.535). Moreover, there is a good deal of controversy over appropriate research methods (Bowling, *et al*, 1993). Consultation may produce results which conflict with managers' views and which are subsequently ignored by them, bringing the process into disrepute. Even the most thoughtful attempts to explore public opinion (Coote, 1993, pp.39-40; Hunter, 1993b, pp.17-18) have experienced difficulties. Members of the public who tried to respond to one such effort (Bowling, *et al*, 1993) were quoted as follows:

> I think we should have everything. It's wrong to make us responsible for grading things (Mature student).

> You need a philosophy degree to fill in this questionnaire. It's ethics, it's impossible (Management consultant). (Both quoted in Tomlin, 1992, p.21.)

Even if the public were willing to make decisions, there would still be dangers (Klein, 1974, pp.408-9), in particular of ignorance about the effects of illnesses and interventions, and of social judgements which might result in allocations based on (say) racism or perceptions of desert. Table 1 sets out the responses of the public, doctors and managers to a question about respondents' relative priorities between ten specified treatments.

Breast cancer screening is highly rated by the public, but much less so by doctors, who are more likely to be aware of its dubious benefits (Hann, 1993). The same may be true of neonatal intensive care. In contrast, the low public ranking of schizophrenia treatment and cancer treatment for smokers suggests a social judgement (Shiu, 1993, p.1048). (For a ranking of different treatment areas, producing the same general response pattern, see Bowling *et al*, 1993, p.853.) As Hunter has noted elsewhere (1993b, p.21), rationing by public consultation alone is likely to be inherently inegalitarian (Freemantle, 1993), and perhaps also inequitable (Bowling *et al*, 1993, p.856.)

## Table 1: Popular Views of Treatment Priorities

*Question*: If you were responsible for prioritising health services, how would you prioritise the things on the list below, in rank order 1 to 10?

| Rank | GENERAL PUBLIC | DOCTORS | MANAGERS |
|---|---|---|---|
| 1 | Childhood Immunisation | Childhood Immunisation | Childhood Immunisation |
| 2 | Screening for breast cancer | Care offered by Gps | 2 = Care offered by Gps; 2 = Education to prevent young smoking |
| 3 | Care offered by Gps | 3 = Support for carers of elderly people; 3 = Education to prevent young smoking | - |
| 4 | Intensive care for premature babies | - | Support for carers of elderly people |
| 5 | Heart transplants | Hip replacement for elderly | Screening for breast cancer |
| 6 | Support for carers of elderly people | Treatment for Schizophrenia | Hip replacement for elderly people |
| 7 | Hip replacement for elderly people | Screening for breast cancer | Treatment for Schizophrenia |
| 8 | Education to prevent young smoking | Intensive care for premature babies | Intensive care for premature babies |
| 9 | Treatment for Schizophrenia | 9 = Heart transplant 9 = Cancer treatment for smokers | Heart transplant |
| 10 | Cancer treatment for smokers | - | Cancer treatment for smokers |

*Source*:    *British Medical Journal*, Vol. 306, 13 March 1993, p.673.

It is possible that Community Health Councils, whose mandate is to represent the public/consumer in the local health policy arena, might be able to find some balance between populism on the one hand and a professionally or managerially driven agenda on the other. This points to a dilemma. There is a view that, despite the significant local authority representation on CHCs, their *public* credibility depends upon their *not* being drawn into discussions about priorities (Bowling *et al*, 1993, p.852). Yet if they are not involved in such discussions, they cannot carry credibility with *other policy-makers* (Davies, 1993, p.14; Association of Community Health Councils in England and Wales, 1993).

### *Central Government*

Central government clearly has a degree of legitimacy in health care rationing, although the way policies are packaged into an election manifesto attenuates any direct link with voters' particular desires. Subject to the general political popularity of the NHS, governments regard themselves as having what might ironically be termed a 'doctor's mandate' in respect of health priorities. For reasons that we have already explored, however, central governments have so far preferred to steer clear of explicit rationing.

### *The Courts*

At least one influential observer, Ian Kennedy, believes the courts will increasingly become involved in health policy and resource allocation decisions (Kennedy, 1993). So far, their role has been minimal and is likely to remain so unless the law concerning the NHS develops greater substantive content. It is difficult to imagine what form this might take, other than a list of services provided by the NHS. If this were to happen, the courts would have a potentially substantial role in interpreting whether new technologies could be included in the list, and whether particular individuals needed any of the listed services. Legislation of this kind would present something of a lottery for policy-makers, a consideration which may well underlie the non-statutory basis of the Conservative government's *Patient's Charter* (Department of Health, 1991).

## Expert Groups

A number of 'expert' groups would wish to play a part in the rationing process. Salter (1992, p.11) has referred to 'open season ... in the needs assessment category of the new political game' created by *Working for Patients*. In practice, however, none of these expert groups claims to make rationing decisions itself. Rather, each offers a preferred paradigm by which decisions ought to be made. Salter (1992, pp.11-13) lists the main groups as follows.

● *Public health physicians'* claims are essentially based on the notion of 'health needs assessment', based on the manipulation of demographic, epidemiological and utilisation data, and a knowledge of the effectiveness of specific health care interventions (see, for instance, Eskin and Bull, 1991, p.17; Hewitson *et al*, 1992).

● *Health economists* employ much of the same data, though with a more tightly specified concept: to maximise health gain for any given level of health care expenditure (see, for instance, Drummond and Maynard's 1993 volume devoted entirely to this topic).

● A number of *health statisticians*, by contrast, are interested in equitable allocations of health service resources at the macro level. They are concerned to develop explicit formulae to serve as proxy for the need for health service *expenditure* in total, rather than with specific medical interventions (see, for an explanation and critique, Sheldon and Carr-Hill, 1991).

● Finally, the proliferation of discussion about rationing health care has invoked the interest of *philosophers* prepared to go beyond the micro question of individual medical ethics (for a review, see Beauchamp and Childress, 1983). Their views are rather less homogeneous and more critical than others we have cited, but raise the question of the criteria by which rationing should take place. For instance Spicker (1993) and Loughlin (1993) have debated the morality of compulsory social solidarity as manifest in third party payment systems for health care, while van Willingenburg (1993) and Zwart (1993) have argued (respectively) that the recent Netherlands health care priority proposals (see below) are over-communitarian and over-libertarian.

### Summary

The *British Medical Journal's* survey endorses much of our analysis of the main players in health service rationing. Table 2 opposite sets out responses to a question about who should make decisions about the relative priority of treatments.

## Table 2: The Players in Rationing Health Care

*Question*: If budgets do need to be set, who should make the decisions on which treatment takes a higher priority?

| | GENERAL PUBLIC % | DOCTORS % | MANAGERS % |
|---|---|---|---|
| Hospital consultants | 61 | 68 | 57 |
| GPs | 49 | 68 | 71 |
| Managers working for local health authorities | 25 | Question not asked | 65 |
| General public | 22 | 30 | 52 |
| Hospital nurses | 19 | 21 | 22 |
| National managers working in the Department of Health | 16 | 23 | 26 |
| Current patients | 9 | 8 | 9 |
| National politicians | 6 | 18 | 36 |
| Local politicians | 3 | 6 | 11 |
| All of the above | 3 | 18 | 21 |
| Don't know | 5 | 2 | - |

*Source*: C Heginbotham.

The general legitimacy of clinical doctors (both consultants and GPs) is extremely high. Managers have a strong view of their own legitimacy, at least at this abstract level, and are the only group to have a strong view of public legitimacy, as well as a reasonably strong view of the legitimacy of national politicians. In general, public opinion favours decision making by doctors, whereas the 'insider' respondents favour a more pluralistic approach.

## CRITERIA FOR RATIONING

The rationing debate has been described as 'curiously muddled and lacking in focus' (Pollock (1993, p.19). Nowhere is this better illustrated than in the discussion of rationing criteria. Public comment upon the birth of sextuplets, as a result of assisted conception, to an unmarried couple, living apart, and with one child already, revealed an interesting mix of values (*Radio Four* 'vox pop', May 1993).

- the couple were unmarried and therefore unstable (and, by implication, immoral), thus presenting an unsuitable prospect for a child's home.

- the couple, though apparently maintaining a stable relationship, lived apart, presenting an unsuitable environment for a child.

- the couple already had one child (by unassisted means) so should not have had priority for assisted conception.

- the cost of welfare benefits for six children would be unacceptably high.

- childlessness is not an illness and therefore assisted conception should not be available on the NHS at all.

This debate, such as it is, exposes a fundamental dilemma of political decision making. On the one hand, the use of implicit criteria helps the world to get along relatively smoothly; as Lindblom seminally observed, it is often easier for players to agree *what* to do rather than *why* they should do it (Lindblom, 1979, p.523). Thus, none of the speakers whose views were paraphrased above would have wished assisted conception to be given to the couple in question. But their very different reasons for withholding treatment have very different policy implications, and represent no common underlying value judgements. This view that implicit criteria may help society to function better has been expanded with specific reference to 'tragic choices' by Calabresi and Bobbitt

(1978), who believe that such decisions should necessarily be hidden from society. Bryan Appleyard has commented: 'The moral choices of rationing health care are too brutal for society to contemplate' (Appleyard, 1992, p.14).

The other horn of the political dilemma is that implicitness can be too easily invoked to conceal unfairness and injustice, to permit special pleading and the pursuit of self-interest under the guise of altruism or public interest. On this view, fair decisions require 'publicity' of the criteria which inform them (Rawls, 1971, p.16; Baker, 1992, p.215).

We shall discuss our own view of the relative merits of the explicitness and implicitness in the concluding section.

## Effectiveness

To the extent that any consistency can be discerned in the debate about rationing criteria, it is to be found in the assertion that 'effectiveness', 'efficacy', 'health gain' or 'ability to benefit' from health care interventions are key concepts. Such assertions seem like commonsense, and indeed from the perspective of one academic discipline (economics), axiomatic criteria; what is the use of treatment that does not work? (McGuire, 1986; Culyer, 1992). This argument can be extended to probable prognoses for particular classes of patient: Ubel *et al* (1993) have argued that, where there are scarcities of organs for transplantation, those available should go to 'first-time' transplant patients on the grounds that mortality is lower than for re-transplanted patients. And there is an argument that, for instance, it is acceptable to discriminate against smokers where the fact of smoking affects the patient's prognosis: 'If you have one heart and several patients needing a transplant, it is only natural that you give it to the patient likely to survive the longest' (Coles, 1993, p.23).

There are, however, at least two serious problems with this view. The first is that, in most cases, we are not dealing with a clear cut question of whether treatment is effective or ineffective. Rather, the questions are *how* effective, and to what degree of probability. These complications are frequently ignored in normative arguments about rationing. Box 5 provides an example.

---

**Box 5**
**An Instrumental View of Health Care**

'Patients seek care in order to be relieved of some actual or perceived, present or potential, "dis-ease". The care itself is not directly of value; it is generally inconvenient, often painful or frightening. As a thought experiment, one could ask a representative patient (or oneself) whether he/she would prefer to have ... a condition perceived as requiring care, plus the best conceivable care for that condition, completely free of all ... costs, or would prefer simply not to have the condition ... care is not a "good"' in the usual sense, but a "bad" or "regrettable", made "necessary" by the even more regrettable circumstances of "dis-ease". It follows that patients want to receive *effective* health care, i.e. care [in respect of which] there is a reasonable expectation [of] a positive impact on their health!'

*Source*: R Evans, 'The Dog in the Night-time: Medical Practice Variations and Health Policy', in T F Andersen and G Mooney, *The Challenge of Medical Practice Variations*; Basingstoke, Macmillan, 1991, pp.118-9.

---

The lacuna in Evans' argument is that players may differ over what constitutes a 'reasonable' expectation of positive impact. Treatments are often provided in the belief, by both doctor and patient, that they *might* (what probability is reasonable?) do *some* good (what amount of 'good' is reasonable?).

A second problem with assertions about effectiveness is that the criteria are often not what they seem. An example can be found in the recent debate about whether coronary artery bypass surgery should be offered to patients who continue to smoke after diagnosis. Those who would withhold such surgery note that smoking has an adverse effect both upon graft survival and on the progression of coronary artery disease; patients who do not, or cease to, smoke therefore have a greater ability to benefit and should be given priority. However, as a recent *British Medical Journal* editorial points out 'The outcome of coronary artery surgery can be compromised by other factors, such as hypertension, diabetes, age, female gender, obesity, and hypercholesterolaemia' (Shiu, 1993, p.1048).

To be consistent, therefore, patients with any combination of factors which is as likely as smoking to reduce their ability to benefit should also be excluded from coronary artery bypass grafting. Yet they are not, even when a factor (such as obesity) is to some extent within the patient's own control. This tendency to 'blame the victim' creeps into rationing advocacy elsewhere, most notably into the assertion that tattoo removal should not be available on the NHS, or should at least be low priority (Harrison and Wistow, 1992, p.124). Yet tattoo removal, like many other 'cosmetic' procedures such as breast augmentation is a highly effective, albeit expensive, procedure (Pollock, 1993, p.19). And there are other inconsistencies in the argument: no-one argues, for instance, that someone injured in a car accident for which he or she is clearly to blame should not be treated.

We cannot, unfortunately, wholly by-pass these problems by deciding that Treatment X is unavailable on the NHS, whilst Treatment Y is available on the NHS to whoever needs it. The problem of judging an individual still arises from the necessity to determine *who* 'needs' the treatment. Expressed more formally, rationing by effectiveness requires the specification of a 'treatment-condition pairing'; one assumes that no-one would prescribe a coronary artery bypass graft for a headache, but there are different degrees of severity of coronary artery disease and those with greater severity are likely to gain more additional years of life from surgery than are those with lesser severity (Williams, 1985). Sometimes, this severity/effectiveness relationship is inverted; low birthweight babies benefit more from neonatal intensive care than do *very* low birthweight babies (Torrance, 1984). It should be noted that the construction of 'condition' categories for treatment/condition pairs is as ethical and political as it is scientific or technical. Suppose, hypothetically, that Treatment Z for people suffering from disease P adds an average of five years to the patient's survival. (Thus, Z/P is the treatment/condition pairing.) But then suppose that the sufferers are sub-divided into, say, those over 65 years old and those under, and that it is then evident that the first group gain only two years additional life on average, whereas the second group averages a gain of ten years. In those terms, Treatment Z is more effective for the under 65s, and the use of a rationing criterion of effectiveness will discriminate against the elderly. Thus ageism can easily be built in, as indeed it is in respect of cervical cytology and breast cancer screening (Jennings, 1993, p.34).

A complex effectiveness based approach has been developed on the west coast of the United States: the so-called Oregon formula. (For brief general accounts, see Dixon and Welch, 1991; Kitzhaber, 1993; Brannigan, 1993; Maynard, 1993). This represents an attempt to provide a set of rules to allow (*inter alia*) all persons below the official poverty line to have access to care under the Medicaid scheme; in order to accomplish this within financial limits acceptable to the Oregon state legislature, the formula seeks to create an effectiveness ranking of treatment/condition pairs upon which a cut-off point for public funding can be determined. Rankings in the Oregon tables have been modified as a result of public consultation, one consequence of which has been to allow social and moral judgements to creep in (Klein, 1992). For example, in the first ranking exercise, liver transplantation necessitated by alcoholic cirrhosis of the liver was ranked 695th in the table (and unlikely to be funded), whereas the same condition without mention of alcohol was ranked 365th (Dixon and Welch, 1991, p.892), and likely to be funded. (This is, in effect, a further demonstration of the point made earlier: defining treatment/condition pairs is as much an ethical and political matter as it is a technical one.)

The Oregon formula passed into state law in 1990, but its implementation was delayed for a long time because it appeared to contravene federal anti-discrimination legislation. The Clinton administration eventually cleared the way for its use (Kitzhaber, p.377), though with modifications in response to some of the criticisms outlined above (Brannigan, 1993, p.32).

## Cost-Effectiveness

The *cost*-effectiveness of a health care intervention might be defined as the cost of one unit of good patient outcome resulting from that intervention. It therefore adds a second dimension to the notion of effectiveness. If the rationing decision is at a micro level, that is, a choice between alternative treatments for the same illness, or a choice between which patients with the same illness should receive a given treatment, then 'patient outcome' can be defined on an *ad hoc* basis. Thus, one might compare different treatments for varicose veins using as an effectiveness criterion whether further treatment was necessary after three years (Piachaud and Weddell, 1972).

But rationing decisions may occur at a macro level, involving choices between quite different treatments for quite different diseases. Cost-effectiveness comparisons in such circumstances require a lowest common denominator concept of effectiveness, for which the main existing candidate is 'utility' to the potential patient, usually defined in terms of additional length of life and/or quality of life gained as a result of the treatment. (Money, of course, serves as a lowest common denominator of cost.) This approach is the foundation of cost-utility analysis, exemplified in the much-discussed calculation of costs per Quality Adjusted Life Year (QALY).

### *Cost-Utility Analysis*

Cost-utility analysis can thus be seen as a special form of cost-effectiveness analysis. Roughly speaking, the calculation of costs per QALY for a health service intervention proceeds along the following lines. (For a fuller explanation, see Gudex, 1986.)

1. Employ medical research literature to identify the expected outcomes for a specified treatment when applied to a specified diagnostic condition. (This is the 'treatment condition pairing' referred to above.) 'Treatment' may just as well be a package of care, or a health promotion intervention, as a surgical operation or pharmaceutical regime.

2.  Translate the expected outcomes into a statement of any
    expected increase in length of life, plus any expected additional
    quality of life. There are several empirically based approaches
    to scaling 'quality of life' (see, for instance, Kind *et al*, 1982),
    and a good deal of contentiousness in the field. There is
    increasing interest in an intended international measure called
    EUROQOL (see European Group 1991). This process provides
    a nett QALY gain expected to result from the treatment; since
    different treatments may produce a different spread of benefits
    over time, it is common practice to 'discount' them so as to
    produce comparable figures (McGuire, *et al*, 1988, pp.81-2).

3.  Divide total costs (discounted if appropriate) of the treatment,
    including any maintenance or follow-up, by the number of
    QALYs expected to be gained. This gives the cost-utility of the
    intervention to the prospective patient, expressed as a number
    of £ per QALY.

The theoretical properties of costs per QALY are as follows.
Suppose that a cost per QALY figure can be given for every
procedure which a specified health system is capable of delivering,
or desires to deliver. A decision rule can then be introduced which
will have the effect of maximising the cost-utility of that health
system, by producing the maximum possible number of QALYs for
any given fixed budget. The rule is to perform as many of the
lowest cost/QALY treatments as is necessary to exhaust the number
of patient cases for whom it is an appropriate treatment, then to treat
as many cases as necessary in the next lowest cost/QALY category,
and so on until the budget is exhausted.

Of course, this is unrealistic in the sense that no real-world health
system would ever be likely to have such data; if it did, strict
adherence to the rule would have the effect of freezing any
developments in medical technology. Advocates of QALYs usually
therefore envisage them as a tool of *marginal analysis*: to help to
decide whether a system should provide more or less of particular
interventions, rather than whether or not to provide them at all
(Mooney *et al*, 1992). It would, of course, be possible to combine

such marginal analysis of existing services with zero-based analysis (i.e. with no presupposition that any will be provided at all) of proposed new ones.

Cost-utility data are usually presented in the form of 'league tables'. Table 3 is an example, compiled from a number of individual studies.

| Table 3: UK Data on Costs and QALYS | £ PER QALY |
|---|---|
| GP advice to stop smoking | 167 |
| Pacemaker implantation for atrioventricular heart block | 700 |
| Hip replacement | 750 |
| Valve replacement for aortic stenosis | 900 |
| CABG for severe angina with LMD | 1,040 |
| CABG for severe angina with 3VD | 1,270 |
| CABG for moderate angina with LMD | 1,330 |
| GP control of hypertension | 1,700 |
| GP control of total serum cholesterol | 1,700 |
| CABG for severe angina with 2VD | 2,280 |
| CABG for moderate angina with 3VD | 2,400 |
| CABG for mild angina with LMD | 2,520 |
| Kidney transplant | 3,200 |
| Breast cancer screening | 3,300 |
| Heart transplant | 5,000 |
| Hospital haemodialysis | 14,000 |

*Source*: *Social Policy Review*, 1988-9, p.115.
*Key*: LMD = left main vessel disease
2/3 VD = 2/3 vessel disease.

The table contains some surprises, in particular the relatively low cost/QALY of cardiac transplantation when compared with, say, hospital renal dialysis.

Cost-utility analysis has been heavily criticised on a number of grounds, and apparently rejected as an option by the present

Secretary of State for Health (Bottomley, 1993, p.4). The criticisms
can be divided into two fairly distinct groups. The first is essentially
a list of caveats about putting QALYs in operation, and in particular
about league tables:

● When using QALYs, it is necessary to clarify the nature of the
  margin that is being used for comparison. In particular, are we
  comparing treatment X with treatment Y, or with no treatment
  at all? What kind of population are we considering extending
  treatment to, and are they more, or less, clinically suitable than
  those patients already in receipt of it? (Drummond, et al, 1993;
  Gerrard and Mooney, 1993; Mooney, et al, 1992.)

● Is the context of the QALY study transferable to that of the
  decision maker? Results obtained by doctors in one location
  may not be matched elsewhere, due to differences between
  doctors, patients and facilities. Costs may also differ widely
  between locations. International comparisons should be treated
  with special caution (Gerrard and Mooney, 1993.)

● How comparable are the cost bases of different QALY studies?
  Do they just include health agencies' costs or are they broader?
  (Drummond, et al, 1993; Gerrard and Mooney, 1993.)

● What is the empirical base of the utility weightings which
  define relative quality of life? Several studies have been based
  on non-random samples of less than 100 respondents.

● Has account been taken of the tendency of respondents to give
  different values to unadjusted years of life at different ages?
  (Gafni and Birch, 1991, p.336.)

● Assuming that the use of a discount rate is appropriate (see
  below), what should that rate be set at? (Drummond, et al,
  1993, p.35).

These caveats all imply a general acceptability of the QALY concept and of cost-effectiveness/cost utility analysis, simply suggesting that they should be used with care. The second group of criticisms is more fundamental, questioning whether the basic approach is of any value.

The single most important of these fundamental criticisms is that the approach entails crudely utilitarian philosophical and political assumptions which are widely questioned. Thus, the maximisation of *total* utility implies nothing about its *distribution* in society, and could (unless supplemented by some other principle of justice) be used to justify actions which would be widely regarded as immoral, such as neglect of the terminally ill (see Körner, 1971, p.136ff). Further, utilitarianism is consequential or 'teleological', in that it judges actions by their (predictable) results, not by their intrinsic moral content; thus it does not allow for an ethical duty to care. We shall look more closely at these 'instrumental' assumptions about health care in the next section.

Another fundamental question concerns *discounting*, that is the principle of reducing the present-day values of costs and benefits which accrue in the future. This principle is a standard feature of microeconomic analysis and is intended to reflect a number of factors including 'myopia' (people are reluctant to think very far ahead), uncertainty (we may not live to enjoy tomorrow's benefits), and the anticipated effects of interest rates and inflation (postponement of consumption is normally rewarded with a positive rate of interest and, because of economic growth, a given cash sum will buy less satisfaction in the future than it will now, even after inflation is allowed for). (For an example of the calculation, see Mooney *et al*, 1980, pp.56-7.) Though these principles are relatively uncontroversial in many contexts, such as the appraisal of business investment plans, their application to benefits in terms of quality and length of life is much disputed, largely because it is not clear that any individual's preferences in these matters will be the same as in other matters (McGuire, *et al*, 1988, pp.97-8; see also Parsonage and Neuberger, 1992).

Other fundamental questions about the cost-utility technique include whether it is feasible to collapse the multi-faceted phenomena of life and its quality onto a single valid scale (Carr-Hill, 1991), whether 'expected utility theory' (upon which cost-utility analysis is founded) is at all valid as a description of people's behaviour when making choices in conditions of uncertainty (Bleichrodt, 1993), whether it is appropriate to ignore the possibility that the act of caring may give utility to the carer or relative too (Bartley, 1993, p.5), and whether analysis of health utilities should be confined to those produced by health services alone, or extended to other policy sectors.

> We are never allowed to ask how many quality adjusted life years could be added to the community by banning nuclear weapons, by improving public transport and housing, or by redistribution of wealth (Bartley, 1993, p.5).

In summary, the costs-per-QALY approach wraps up into an ostensibly technical formula a variety of ethical and political judgements to which we may or may not subscribe. (For an entertaining, but serious, sociological analysis of this, see Mulkay *et al*, 1987).

Curiously, QALY league tables, much as they have been debated, and despite having at least some support within the medical profession (see, for instance, Grimes 1987; Petrou and Renton 1993), do not seem so far to have found their way into explicit health care rationing decisions in the UK, though the same sort of logic, in the form of disability-adjusted life years (DALYs) has been taken up by the World Bank (World Bank, 1993).

## Non-instrumental Criteria

Effectiveness, cost-effectiveness and cost-utility are all examples of an *instrumental* approach to rationing, that is, they assume that health services are valued only for the positive effects that they have on people's health status. Although well on the way to being ubiquitous in policy making circles (see, for instance, Bottomley, 1993, p.11; Advisory Group on Health Technology Assessment, 1992, p.8), this stance should not be taken as *axiomatically* desirable. Since our concern is with the publicly-funded NHS of the UK, the point can be demonstrated with reference to Goodin and Wilenski's (1984) analysis of the role of instrumentality in public policy generally. The essentials of their argument are as follows.

First, people's values are as much concerned with *means* as with ends. Consider society's general willingness to approve of rescue attempts for sailors and climbers, or other heroic lifesaving feats, in circumstances where the chances of success are extremely low: we are pleased that 'they did everything they could.' Second, if a service is publicly funded and if (to some extent) the purpose of government is to respond to people's preferences, then it follows that government policies should be judged as much by their content as by their impact. And indeed, so they are.

It is easy to transfer this argument to the specific context of health care. It would justify the public provision of services with a low probability of successful patient outcome, or indeed those where outcomes are difficult to specify or observe. For instance, it would justify the provision of an expensive new drug of dubious efficacy to a patient with an almost certainly fatal condition. (For an account of the much-publicised dispute over the attempted prescription of Interleukin 2 to a patient at the Christie Hospital in Manchester, see Freemantle and Harrison, 1994; for a discussion of Islamic medical ethics of 'making an effort', see Haleem, 1993, p.17.) This is a weak version of what Dworkin (1994, p.22) has referred to as the 'rescue principle': that everything should be sacrificed in order to preserve life and health.

A problem with such a non-instrumental approach is that it may carry large *opportunity costs*: perhaps, for instance, more lives could have been saved had the money been spent on other services instead. In theory, the technique of cost-benefit analysis allows for the assessment of *all* costs and *all* benefits of an activity, irrespective of to whom they accrue (McGuire *et al*, 1988, p.75). In practice, such analysis is rarely feasible: it would require knowledge of, and the assignment of monetary values to, all costs and benefits, with little prospect of the valuation being uncontentious. Even if it were applied, it would merely guarantee that the total 'welfare' of society were maximised. Unless some further adjustment were made for 'equity' (see below), it would not guarantee any particular *distribution* of welfare (McGuire et al, 1988, p.89).

The political ideology of such non-instrumental approaches is ambiguous. The underlying notion that the purpose of the state is to satisfy citizens' expectations is an essentially liberal democratic stance, leading to a view of the citizen as consumer, and to the market as the best way of satisfying their needs (Doyal and Gough, 1991, p.10). On the other hand, as Titmuss observed from a different political perspective in his seminal study of blood donation *The Gift Relationship* (Titmuss, 1973), the act of attempting to help those in need is itself a unifying and civilising force (see also Fuchs, 1974, p.134). Of course, it may be that public opinion on such matters would be modified if more information about the costs and effectiveness of treatments were available, but this is by no means certain. Moreover, questions about the effectiveness of treatments are largely about degrees of probability rather than certain cures or clear uselessness.

Another non-instrumental criteria is entitlement, that is, perceived fairness in relation to past contributions to the NHS. A 62-year-old Wakefield man denied arterial surgery on grounds that he had been unable to cease smoking was quoted as saying

> I have worked since I was fourteen up until recently and paid a hell of a lot in taxes to the government both in income taxes and on the 40 cigarettes a day I smoked. Surely it is not too much for me to ask to have an operation that might ease my pain in my old age and make me live a little longer (*Yorkshire Evening Post*, 26 August 1993, p.1).

## 'Fair Goes'

There is a long-standing and respectable philosophical position that, in certain circumstances, the action of chance, that is, random selection provides a just outcome in the distribution of scarce benefits. (For a detailed exposition of justice by lottery, see Goodwin, 1992a.) Boyd *et al* (1979, pp.76-7) noted that supporters of the 'clinical argument' (see Box 1) relied partly on the assumption that elements of chance operated in determining the 'first come' who were 'first served'. More recently, Doyal (1993, p.53) has argued that health care above a universal entitlement level could be distributed in this manner.

An alternative concept of 'fair goes' is that a recipient of unsuccessful treatment should go to the end of the queue before further attempts at treatment are made. At least one health authority has introduced such a procedure for IVF (*NHSME News*, No. 72, August, 1993, p.10). The underlying assumption is that such an arrangement would only be fair where the treatment had been competently given.

## Need

Rationing by 'need' is a more obviously socialist approach to resource allocation in health care than the criteria discussed above (Goodwin, 1992b, p.341). An immediate problem is to distinguish between 'need' and 'demand', since the former term is often used rhetorically, as a means of occupying the moral high ground in political debate. But if the two could be distinguished, then it might be possible to employ need as a criterion for deciding which demands should and should not be met, and indeed to determine what services should be provided even though they have not been demanded.

In their widely acclaimed book *A Theory of Human Need*, Doyal and Gough have made this distinction, seeing needs as the essential preconditions for human action and interaction (1991, p.50).

Although the book is pitched at a broad conceptual level, it is highly relevant to our topic, since it defines people's basic needs as, firstly, survival and physical health and, secondly 'autonomy' of individuals to formulate and pursue aims and strategies which they believe to be in their interests (p.59) - a concept which includes mental health (p.61). Failure to have such objective needs met constitutes social injustice which socialists should strive to avoid and to remedy (pp.1-2). This is an *instrumental* concept of need, that is, it is a means to some end, in this case life, health and autonomy (Culyer, 1992, p.12). Doyal and Gough do not, of course, imply that health services are the sole or main means for fulfilling these basic needs. But 'need' only provides a partial criterion for rationing, since what is medically possible (to mention only one vehicle for meeting these needs) may well exceed what a government or society is willing to pay for (Dworkin, 1994, p.22).

## Equity

The notion of 'equity' is developed from that of needs, implying both equal treatment for those with equal needs, and a consistent relationship between the extent of people's needs and the extent of their treatment; this therefore constitutes both 'vertical' and 'horizontal' equity. In the context of welfare services, 'An equitably distributed service is one in which only variables which measure [people's] needs for the service provide a significant explanation of whether [they] receives the service' (Evandrou *et al*, 1992, p.489).

These definitions are, however, insufficient for operational purposes; in order to apply them to real rationing situations and to develop policies with a substantive content we have both to define what is to count as 'treatment' and (since it is impractical for policy-makers to compare every individual citizen's needs with every other's) define what social groups are to be compared.

In the field of health care, we might for instance be concerned with the distribution of health expenditure, or of different grades of health professional, or of CT scanners. This is to employ health service *inputs* as the definition of treatment. Alternatively, we might be concerned with the distribution of *processes*, or access to health care; how equitable, for instance is the distribution of coronary artery bypass graft surgery? A third alternative is to be concerned with health service *outcome*, or some proxy for it, such as mortality or disability. These three alternatives correspond roughly to Le Grand's (1982) concepts of equity of access, utilisation and outcome respectively. Of course, all these categories can be subdivided into far more detailed operational ideas.

Just as there are choices about how to define 'treatment', so there are choices about what social groups to compare. A non-exhaustive list of possibilities would include socioeconomic groups, age cohorts, gender, ethnic groups, diagnostic categories, and geographical areas; there may be relationships between these groups, though not always obvious ones (Macintyre *et al*, 1983).

As Figure 3 shows, there are a great many ways of defining equity in health care: 18 in total, and that is without being very detailed on either of the dimensions! Studies of equity of health services may be concerned with any of the cells in Figure 3, but numbers 3 (see, for instance, Townsend and Davidson, 1983), 5 (see, for instance, Evandrou *et al*, 1992), 16 (see, for instance, Clarke *et al*, 1993) and 18 (see, for instance, Macintyre *et al*, 1993) are common foci of interest.

## Figure 3
### Alternative Definitions of Equity in Health Care

|  |  | Currency of 'treatment' | | |
|  |  | Inputs | Processes | Outcomes |
|---|---|---|---|---|
|  | Social Classes | 1 | 2 | 3 |
| Social Groups | Age Groups | 4 | 5 | 6 |
| for comparison | Gender | 7 | 8 | 9 |
|  | Ethnic Groups | 10 | 11 | 12 |
|  | Diagnostic categories | 13 | 14 | 15 |
|  | Geography | 16 | 17 | 18 |

Despite recent initiatives (*Local Voices*: NHS Management Executive, 1992) concerning the needs of small geographical areas, government interest in health care equity has for the last 20 years been entirely confined to the matter of financial resource distribution between Health Authorities, that is, the 'RAWP' formula (Resource Allocation Working Party 1976; for a critique see, for instance, Sheldon and Carr-Hill, 1992). It is easy to see why this is so; equity is a complex objective which it is difficult to pursue with the blunt policy instruments of central control. At least one local hospital management has attempted to achieve equity among *individuals* awaiting treatment. Salisbury Hospital has been reported as piloting a scheme under which non-emergency patients are given a score ranging from 0 to 4 points on each of five variables: speed of progression of the disease, pain and distress, disability and dependence on others, loss of employment, and time on the waiting list. Priority might be given to those with the highest score in any one category, and might lead to patients with low scores not being placed on the list at all (Giles, 1993, p.7).

Equity and efficiency may conflict with each other. Policies aimed at maximising benefits to a whole society will not necessarily produce the most equitable *distribution* of those benefits within that society (Culyer, 1992, p.13; Mooney *et al*, 1992, pp.9, 18). However, it is possible to give the highest priority to equity objectives and then seek to maximise benefits within that constraint (McGuire, 1986, p.1173; Culyer, 1992, p.13).

What are in effect rough guidelines for such an approach have been distilled by Light (1991) from the work of Cochrane (1972). Figure 4 opposite sets out a version of this, adapted to give equity clear priority.

It is also possible for the two central facets of 'need', physical health and autonomy, to conflict with one another. How are we to regard the need for health brought about by autonomously chosen health-damaging behaviour? One answer to this is exclude from consideration inequalities in health brought about by such behaviour:

---

**Figure 4**
**Decisions in Pursuit of Equity of**
**Survival & Physical Health**

1.  Prevent what ill-health is preventable by
    - healthy public policy
    - social medicine (e.g. vaccinations)

2.  Consider all effective treatments/interventions. Give
    priority to those which are most likely to have the
    effect of equalising mortality and morbidity across
    social groups. Make treatments that are prioritised
    available and accessible to all who are likely to benefit.

3.  Within 2 above provide for any specific health care
    needs only the most cost-effective treatments in the
    most cost-effective settings (e.g. day surgery where
    appropriate), at the most cost-effective stage in the
    disease process (i.e. usually early). (Note that this
    approach does not require lowest-common denominator
    measures of effectiveness.)

*Source*: Adapted from D.W. Light 'Effectiveness and efficiency
under competition: the Cochrane Test', *British Medical Journal*,
Vol.303, pp.1253-4, 1991.

---

Equity in health implies that ideally everyone should have
a *fair opportunity* to attain their full health potential and
.... that none should be disadvantaged from achieving this
potential if it can be avoided (Whitehead, 1992, p.433,
emphasis original).

An alternative answer, which avoids the danger of 'victim-blaming',
is to acknowledge that people need to sustain and improve their
physical health and autonomy *over time* (Doyal and Gough, 1991,
p.55). This implies that someone whose health is impaired by (say)
a skiing accident or freely chosen drug abuse still has a need for
health. Such decisions, which address the need for equity of
autonomy, are not very susceptible to expert, technical decision-

making and therefore present a number of operational difficulties -
a point well illustrated by a report for the Dutch Government
(Government Committee on Choices in Health Care, 1992).

Recognising the necessity for rationing services under the basic
national scheme of social insurance, this report argues that the
scheme should provide care that is 'necessary' to assist people to
function normally (p.49). Thus, it acknowledges equity as a
criterion. However, it notes three different perspectives on normal
functioning. First, there is the *individual* perspective in which no
distinction is made between need and demand and which (as we saw
at the beginning of this paper) cannot be used to make decisions at
a macro level (p.51). Second, there is the *medical professional*
perspective, which focuses on 'normal species-typical' function,
though often to the exclusion of psycho-social functioning. From
this perspective, necessary care is that which prevents and removes
dangers to life and/or enhances normal function as defined above
(p.52). Third, there is the *community* perspective, which envisages
normal functioning as 'the ability of every member of society to
participate in social life' (p.54); necessary care is that which
enhances such participation. The Report's recommendations are
summarised in Figure 5 opposite.

The report argues that the third, community, perspective should
predominate, but that, within its limits, the medical professional
perspective should operate, whilst, within the limits of the latter, the
individual perspective should operate (p.55). This proposed
hierarchy of priority is not, however, coherent. The medical
professional perspective is, in fact, the narrowest of the three and is
therefore unlikely to include anything not covered by the broader
community perspective. The implication of the hierarchy as
proposed is simply that the doctor can only offer services available
on the basic insurance scheme, and that the patient can only choose
between services offered by the doctor. The report further argues
that, in addition to being 'necessary' in the sense described above,
care available in the basic insurance package should be effective,
efficient, and of a kind that would not more appropriately be left to
individual responsibility. The import of the last criterion is

---

**Figure 5**
**Rationing Criteria Proposed to the Dutch Government**

1.     Is the care necessary

      (a)    to enhance the individual's participation in
            social life?

      (b)    If so, will the care remove danger to life
            and/or enhance biological function?

      (c)    If so, does the individual desire the care?

2.     If the above are satisfied, is the care effective?

3.     If so, is the care efficient?

4.     If so, is the care something which could not be left to
      individual responsibility?

*Summarised from*: *Choices in Health Care*, A Report by the
Government Committee on Choices in Health Care; Rijswijk, The
Netherlands, 1992.

---

somewhat unclear, since it is explicitly stated that such criteria as age and unhealthy lifestyle would not be employed as rationing criteria (pp.84-6).

Despite occasional lack of clarity in analysis, some of which we have pointed out above, the Dutch proposals can be seen as offering a possible approach to equity of autonomy as well as to equity of survival and physical health. There are, however, problems of operationalisation; any purported rationing criteria must be able to discriminate between health care that enhances autonomy and physical health and that which does not. The Dutch report proposes that IVF be excluded from the basic package on the grounds that childlessness does not interfere with normal social functioning in Holland (p.87). Yet, childlessness is clearly a social dysfunction *for some people* and at least one critic has concluded that the community perspective on needs is fatally flawed (Van Willigenburg, 1993, p.50).

This seems to us to miss the point. Whilst it may (or may not) be true that Dutch society is generally unconcerned about childlessness, no light is shed on this by individual cases. One can always suppose that, for any personal attribute, there is an individual who finds it dysfunctional. It would be more useful to consider the proportion of Dutch people whose normative expectations were that couples should have children. This could be taken as a crude proxy for the severity of social dysfunction likely to be caused by childlessness. (In a recent survey, 51 percent of *British* men and 41 of British women agreed that 'a marriage without children is not complete', a higher figure than for the USA or Germany (*The Guardian*, 1 December, 1993).)

A recent and novel approach to the problem of defining equity (or 'justice' in his term) in health care provision has been proposed by Dworkin (1994, pp.22-3). Dworkin begins with a thought experiment in which, first, wealth and income were more widely distributed than at present, second, information about the costs and effectiveness of health care were generally public, and third, there was no basis on which to predict a particular person's probable future health experience. In such an imaginary situation there would be no need for state intervention in the health care arena; individuals would have the financial means and the information upon which to base personal decisions about an appropriate quantity of health insurance cover; at the same time, insurance companies would have no basis for relating premia to an individual's risk of ill-health. All this Dworkin terms the 'prudent insurance' ideal. He notes that, since the thought experiment is unlikely to be translated into the real world situation, the 'prudent insurance' concept of equity can only be introduced if policy makers use the thought experiment as the basis for defining a basic health care package.

*Some* elements of such a policy are predictable, according to Dworkin. It would be unlikely that life-sustaining treatment for those in a persistent vegetative state would be funded; likewise for those with irreversible dementia and where it seemed unlikely that treatment would extend the life of an elderly person by more than a few weeks. The basis of these predictions is simply that hardly anyone would judge it worth paying the insurance premia necessary to fund such treatment. (It seems more probable that it would be judged prudent to insure for, say, pain relief and other services to keep a dying person comfortable.)

What the Dworkin principle provides, if it can be brought into practice, is horizontal equity of process. People with the same health problems would be treated similarly, that is, given treatments that were known in general terms to be effective for their particular condition, but without regard to social factors. The difficulties in putting the principle into practice would be considerable, both because of the complexities (noted above) of defining treatment/condition pairings and because of uncertainties about the appropriate players and mechanisms for performing the 'thought experiment'.

It should be recognised that equity of *process*, as envisaged above, will not necessarily produce equity of *outcome*. Indeed health *care* might not be the most significant policy variable when compared with socio-economic conditions, environmental factors and lifestyles (Whitehead, 1992, p.433; Doyal and Gough, 1991, chaps 10, 11). The clear implication, to which we shall return, is that equitable health outcomes require more equitable public policies in general.

This does not mean that equitable health *care* is unimportant; health care can save lives and improve physical health. Moreover, health care which is no more than palliative can still be perceived as effective in enhancing social solidarity between citizens as both payers for, and receivers of, care. Since feelings of (for instance) helplessness and worthlessness are part of a broad conception of mental illness (Doyal and Gough, 1991, pp.63-4), it follows that caring actions arising from social solidarity can be one contribution to people's basic need for autonomy.

## The Criteria: Concluding Comments

What then are the appropriate criteria for rationing health care? Our own view is that such criteria should be concerned with some form of equality and at the same time with autonomy. This is not just because we live in a more individualistic society than perhaps ever before, but because equity and autonomy are logically and conceptually closely interrelated (Lukes, 1973, p.124). Equality does not simply mean that persons are, or should be, the same (clearly neither is the case) but that persons should be entitled to equal respect as human beings and equal life chances.

> .... entitlement to social goods is .... a way of strengthening and deepening democracy. Rights [including] health care .... are regarded as essential components of citizenship, because these things make it possible for individuals to exercise their civil and political rights, and more generally to participate in society. According to this view, democratic society depends upon the *just distribution of social goods* - which should be a matter of right, not privilege (Coote, 1993, p.1, emphasis added).

In terms of health care, it seems to us that the consequence is that the pursuit of *equity* (i.e. equal treatment for equal needs) is the overriding objective. Moreover, Doyal and Gough's (1991) designation of survival/physical health and autonomy (including, it will be recalled, mental health) as the most basic of objective human needs is highly consonant with this position. The question than arises of how we are to operationalise the notion of equity in health care. In our view there are two quite different principles at stake and policy makers must seek some balance between them.

First, there is the relatively straightforward principle of *equity of survival and physical health*. This clearly implies that access to *effective* health care *processes* should be provided on an equitable (including accessible) basis, and that a healthy public policy should be pursued more generally in areas such as the environment, transport and housing. Such a policy would be knowledge-based, it would eschew social judgements as the basis of treatment or service provision, and it would not involve large-scale populist consultation exercises such as that undertaken by the *British Medical Journal* (see below), and some Health Authorities.

Second, there is the much more diffuse principle of *equity of autonomy*. Some implications are clear, for instance that there would be an important role for equitably distributed information and education about health/ill-health and their causes. Mental health services, care of the physically disabled, assisted conception and services for those with learning difficulties could be provided on much the same basis as Figure 4, except that effectiveness would be judged by the consequent increase in recipients' autonomy (Doyal and Gough, 1991, pp.61-6). There would probably have to be services whose main justification was non-instrumental, in that they symbolised social solidarity and 'doing our best' for people. These would include care (without its being the pretence of 'cure') for people who were acutely ill without hope of recovery. Some decisions taken accordingly would be painful and hotly-contested, such as whether to prescribe expensive drugs with only a remote prospect of affecting a fatal condition (Freemantle and Harrison, 1993).

In addition, policy should take account of other implications of the analysis offered in earlier sections of this report. These would include: sufficient flexibility to maintain a sense of social solidarity (Fuchs, 1974, p.134; Fishkin, 1979); 'due process' of decision making so as to provide for the political legitimisation of health care rationing decisions (Klein, 1993, p.310); efficient provision and management of services to minimise opportunity costs; and the co-ordination of decision making between the health and the NHS, and other policy sectors which impact on health.

In the final section of this paper, we explore two particular options for public policy which might help to create favourable conditions for implementing these ideas. There are some choices within each broad approach. Our analysis is not exhaustive and its various elements could doubtless be combined in different ways.

## OPTIONS FOR PUBLIC POLICY

The policy proposals which follow are presented as *scenarios*. Our aim is to give a flavour about how two particular constellations of options might work together. To some extent, this has the effect of polarising our ideas and in our concluding comments we draw attention to the most significant of these polarities. But we do not wish to suggest that there is a straight choice between our two scenarios. Some combination of them is perfectly feasible.

### Scenario I: Local Democratic Representation

The core of scenario I is the delegation to local government authorities of responsibility for the NHS. The authorities would become *purchasers* of health care, perhaps from the same range of providers - NHS Trusts and (occasionally) private healthcare organisations - from whom the present District Health Authorities purchase (for an outline, see Harrison *et al*, 1990, pp.169-74). The idea of greater local authority involvement in health care is, of course, not a new one. Much pre-NHS health care was provided in this way (Watkin, 1978, pp.8-10), and the proposal was revived by Regan and Stewart (1982) a decade or so ago. The more specific notion of local government authorities as purchasers, rather than providers, of health care was proposed by the present authors more recently in an IPPR report (Harrison, *et al*, 1991; see also Harrison 1992, Wistow 1993); the matter has since become more widely debated. Indeed, one London borough council has actually written to the Secretary of State for Health proposing

> the transfer to the Council of the responsibility for the purchasing of, initially, primary and community health care, and ultimately acute care as well (Wandsworth Borough Council, 1993, p.11).

The idea has the support of the Association of Metropolitan Authorities (1993a,b), as well as the President of the Institute of Health Services Management. Weaker versions of the scheme, involving elected *ad hoc* authorities of various forms have been proposed from time to time (Ham 1985, Paton 1993, Ashton *et al* 1992), as have joint purchasing commissions between local authorities and health authorities (Martin, *et al*, 1993).

The local government scenario in principle offers three important benefits to health policy. First, it provides a direct democratic input: in the context of this paper, democratic legitimacy for rationing decisions. We return below to the question of what rationing criteria might be employed. Second, it offers, though does not *guarantee* (Mays, 1993), full integration of health and social care planning and purchasing, ending the present artificial division between the two, and the perverse incentives generated by it. Third, it brings health *treatment* and care into a policy arena which includes other important determinants of health. Environmental health, local roads and traffic, and public housing are all still substantially regulated by local government authorities. (In order to emphasise this necessity for integration, our earlier report for IPPR proposed that overall responsibility for health policy be transferred to the Department of the Environment.)

The latter two advantages are relatively uncontentious (see, for instance, *The Financial Times*, 6 June 1991, p.12). More problematic is the core ideal of local democracy. Arguments against local democracy fall into two categories, both recently employed by the National Association of Health Authorities and Trusts in its recent discussion paper *Securing Effective Public Accountability in the NHS* (NAHAT, 1993; see also Hunt, 1993).

The first argument is essentially that local government is not really democratic at all, being both over-politicised and over-bureaucratised with important decisions being made by Councillors, and a correspondingly reduced role for managers (NAHAT, 1993, p.14). This is a contradictory argument, surely: the fact that Councillors take decisions (if they do) makes local government more, rather than less democratic. It also fails to take account of the undemocratic nature of central government, which would otherwise continue to control health policy: the British constitution provides for the continued dominance of the Executive over the legislature, and, as Stewart (1992) has argued, democracy consists of little more than periodic general elections.

The second group of arguments, also employed by NAHAT (1993, p.11) is that local government control would undermine the national character of the NHS by introducing local variance in the range of services provided. This, of course, is precisely the point of Scenario I and can be seen as both a strength and a weakness. Different services, especially if coupled with decentralised revenue raising (such as local income tax) could lead to competition between localities in the form of 'fiscal migration' (Boyne, 1992; Dunleavy and O'Leary, 1987, p.120; Weale, 1983, p.187, see also Bogdanor, 1992). This would certainly enhance the need for a system of allocating central government grants to local authorities which fully reflected the social class structure and deprivation patterns of local populations. There is no particular reason to believe that present day local government authorities (counties and metropolitan districts) are too small for such a role (Eminson, 1991, p.8), although this point has been explicitly argued by NAHAT and is the implicit assumption behind the current NHS trend towards merging purchasing authorities. Over the last 15 years, local government has seen its role cut back by central government and its status reduced (partly as a result of its own behaviour). Scenario I could breathe new life and political salience into local government by giving it powers to take decisions which would be seen locally as important. In putting forward this option we acknowledge that nothing less than a new model of governance would be required. This would have major implications not just for the NHS but also for local government, particularly regarding political structures and processes.

If local authorities were entirely free to choose their own criteria for rationing health care, there is no certainty that they would all pursue equity. There is, moreover, some force in the view that a degree of national consistency is desirable in a country as small as the UK. Our scenario therefore includes two statutory constraints upon local government decision making for health and social care.

The first would prohibit the use of purely social judgements (about lifestyle, for instance) in establishing entitlement to services or treatments. This prohibition could be expressed in contracts between local authority purchasers and providers of care. The second constraint would be a much more general statutory duty to pursue equity of outcome (in terms of survival and physical health as well as autonomy) through integrated local policies for health, environment, education and other relevant areas. Figure 4 above would suggest an appropriate strategic approach, if it were extended to cover autonomy as well as survival and physical health. It seems unlikely that *detailed* legislation would be an appropriate vehicle for establishing this second duty, but it could be employed as a criterion in Audit Commission evaluations of local authorities.

Within these broad constraints, local authorities would remain free to ration health care in a variety of ways. Some might choose to establish specific local health care rights for individuals resident in the district, whereas others might prefer to establish broader objectives, within which waiting lists and clinical freedom would dispense rough justice (Boyd *et al*, 1979, p.76; Doyal, 1993, p.53; Hunter, 1993a, p.51). This what Hunter (1993a, p.28) has termed 'muddling through elegantly'.

## Scenario II: National Health Care Rights

The basic assumption of scenario II is that it is desirable and practicable to establish, at national level, a set of explicit health care rights, based on equity of process within the limits of an agreed health care package. People with specified needs would thus have rights to receive care and/or treatment aimed at meeting those needs. From this perspective, health care needs can be identified, and services rationed, in much the same way that dietary needs were identified, and foodstuffs rationed, in the 1939-45 war (Bartley, 1993, p.6). In our scenario, such rights would be statutorily based, and therefore quite different from both the present *Patient's Charter* (DoH, 1991) and the present legal basis of the NHS as outlined above (Dimond 1993; Coote 1993, pp.45-6; Salter 1992).

There are various ways in which such entitlements might be delivered. This scenario (unlike scenario I) would not *necessarily* require a continued purchaser/provider split. If the statutory rights were enforceable against district health authorities, their funding would have to be based upon an actuarial assessment of the incidence of the relevant needs in each specific local government population, and an assessment of the probable costs of relevant care and treatment. This would be similar to the situation facing the State of Oregon; if the actual numbers of cases exceeded the actuarial estimate, government (central government in the UK case) would have to provide the additional resources (Dixon and Welch, 1991).

In the context of UK public expenditure, this would mean that financing the NHS would begin to resemble the financing of social security in that it would no longer be largely cash-limited. (For an explanation of the present system of cash limits in government expenditure, see Thain and Wright, 1991.) This would be wholly unattractive to any central government committed to tight public expenditure control, unless the statutory rights were *minimum* rights, leaving district health authorities some financial 'headroom' to spend on services not covered by statute. Since statutory rights would need a fair degree of specificity in order to be enforceable, they might well be expressed as 'treatment/condition pairings' (see above). In practice, therefore, it is likely that greater weight would be given to equity of survival/physical health than to equity of autonomy. It should also be recognised that medical conditions are not absolutely objective, and that 'diagnosis shifting' (Hunter, 1993a, pp.25-6) or 'priority creep' (Meek, 1992, p.16) may well occur; in other words, doctors may sometimes alter their diagnosis in order to allow a patient to be treated within the rationing criteria.

Scenario II, by virtue of its basis in *statutory* rights would derive the legitimacy of its rationing criteria from the sanction of Parliament. However, a considerable amount of detailed work would have to be undertaken in order to specify the treatment/condition pairings and (in our view) to give them some additional legitimacy based in public opinion. One vehicle for the oversight of this process (which would have to be an ongoing one in order to keep pace with developments in medical technology) would be a Standing Royal Commission. Such a body would need to undertake empirical research into public opinion. Rather than the kind of simple opinion polling whose results were outlined in an earlier section of this paper, our scenario includes a public consultation process with two key features.

First, it would be based upon an attempt to apply the 'prudent insurance' principle outlined above. We are not aware of any empirical attempt to establish whether in fact there is homogeneity of public opinion upon such matters. (It seems likely, for instance, that different individuals will display different degrees of risk-aversion.) Nevertheless, there may well be sufficient homogeneity to provide the basis of at least minimum rights and to provide (as Dworkin himself speculates: 1994, p.23) a few clear exclusions of expensive and relatively ineffective treatments.

Second, the methodology for obtaining public opinion would have to entail considerable depth of discussion in order for Dworkin's 'thought experiment' to be conducted successfully. Non-populist consultation exercises have previously been attempted, though not with the specific objective that we have proposed here. Box 6 gives an outline of the kind of mechanism that might be employed.

---

**BOX 6**
**NON-POPULIST PUBLIC CONSULTATION**
**- AN EXAMPLE FROM LEEDS**

The auditing team at Leeds Metropolitan University applied the theoretical framework developed by [Doyal and Gough, 1991]. They set out to test a particular method of auditing, as well as to find out how people in the targeted area of Leeds articulated their needs. Their work involved a lengthy postal questionnaire to a random sample of local residents (eliciting a response amounting to 10 per cent of the total population); a large number of in-depth interviews with selected individuals who had filled in the questionnaire, as well as interviews with local service workers and others with relevant local expertise; and a thorough review of national and local statistics. The auditing team then compiled a draft report which sought to integrate knowledge of local citizens with the normative knowledge of experts and service workers. A short version of this report was circulated in the community where the audit took place and, finally, a series of open meetings were held, at which local people were invited to discuss the way the team had processed their findings.

*Source*: A Coote, 'Public participation in decisions about health care', *Critical Public Health*, Vol. 4, No. 1, p.40, 1993.

---

Another possibility being explored by IPPR at the time of writing is to apply the jury principle, with citizens selected at random from the electoral register being empanelled locally for a finite period, to deliberate on the contents and boundaries of a basic health care package (Stewart, forthcoming).

Scenario II is concerned with health care rather than with health. That is because defining rights to health, as opposed to health care, would be an extremely difficult task, and enforcing rights would be all but impossible. (For a discussion of rights to health see Benton, 1994, forthcoming.)

## CONCLUDING COMMENTS

Our two scenarios are not intended to be mutually exclusive. They could complement each other, the first operating within a framework defined by the second. If policy-makers are to decide whether to introduce either one of them, or to combine the two - and, if so, exactly how this is to be done - it will be important to consider the following issues.

### Centralisation

Scenario I is as decentralised as is likely to be practicable in Britain. It makes a virtue of the possibility of differences in service provision between different localities, albeit within a national strategic framework. Scenario II reflects assumptions that people want a truly nationalised and consistent service. These possibilities cannot, of course, be isolated from the more general political debate about the relative roles of central and local government.

### Integration

Scenario I places considerable emphasis on integration of public services generally, and particularly of those that impact upon health and autonomy. Scenario II singles out health *care* as the subject of statutory rights.

### Explicitness

Since the form of Scenario I does not of itself determine the rationing criteria likely to be employed, it will be possible for either explicit or implicit ones to develop. However, the context of political choices could be more explicit if they were based in a new form of local government. Scenario II by definition requires explicit statements.

*Physical Health Care or More?*

Scenario I will not bring wholly predictable results, but it is possible that a very wide range of objectives, including 'autonomy' and embracing holistic notions of health, would underlie rationing decisions. Scenario II, whilst it provides for residual expenditure on broad objectives, is narrower in its focus and is clearly built around rights to health care for the purposes of survival and physical health.

*Organisational Change*

Scenario I necessarily entails quite radical organisational change on the purchaser side of the NHS though little on the provider side. Scenario II does not *require* any substantial organisational change, but could, if introduced on its own, permit a new integration of the purchaser and provider functions.

It is undoubtedly possible to select and combine elements from both scenarios. As we have suggested, one such combination would involve nationally-determined statutory rights to individual health care enforceable by local government authorities, who would be responsible for purchasing not only services to meet specific health care entitlements, but also services to meet other, locally-determined, non-statutory priorities. This third scenario combines some of the strengths of I and II, but carries a risk that if health *care* alone were subject to statutory rights, particular services would be privileged at the expense of others which may be no less important in pursuing the goals of health and autonomy for all. This problem might be diminished if rights to health care were supplemented by other social rights, for example, to housing. However the difficulties of introducing any substantive (as opposed to procedural) rights are considerable. (For a fuller discussion of this point, see Coote 1992, p.7-9, and forthcoming). The strength and appeal of Scenario I is that any bias towards health care can more easily be countered by a focus on the broader determinants of health.

There is much further work to be done in exploring these scenarios and their components, and in providing greater detail about how they would work in practice. Our purpose has been to contribute to the construction of a robust policy towards the rationing of health care by mapping a course of deliberation which policy makers might usefully follow.

# REFERENCES

**Aaron H J & Schwartz W B** (1984), *The Painful Prescription: Rationing Hospital Care*, Washington DC, Brookings Institution.

**Advisory Group on Health Technology Assessment** (1992), *Assessing the Effects of Health Technologies: Principles, Practice, Proposals*, London, Department of Health.

**Appleyard B** (1992), 'High cost of dying', *The Times*, 8 July, p.14.

**Arrow K J** (1963), 'Uncertainty and the economics of medical care', *American Economic Review*, Vol. 53, pp.941-73.

**Ashburner L & Cairncross L** (1993), 'Membership of the 'new style' health authorities: continuity or change?', *Public Administration*, Vol. 71, No. 3, pp.357-75.

**Ashton J, Booth C, Brunt J, Colin-Thome D, Conrad J, Jenkins S, Lye M, Newton P & Shakespeare G** (1992), *Caring for the Community in the 21st Century*, Manchester, University of Manchester Health Services Manager Centre.

**Association of Community Health Councils in England and Wales** (1993), Rationing Health Care: Should CHCs Help?, London.

**Association of Metropolitan Authorities** (1993a), Local authorities and health services: notes of a meeting to discuss the future role of local government and the provision, purchasing and promotion of health services in England and Wales: 14 July, London.

**Association of Metropolitan Authorities** (1993b), *Local Authorities and Health Services: A Future Role for Local Authorities in the Purchasing of Health Services: A Scoping Paper*, London.

**Baker R** (1992), 'The inevitability of health care rationing: a case study of rationing in the British National Health Service' in M A Strosberg, J M Weiner, R Baker & I A Fein (Eds), *Rationing America's Medical Care: the Oregon Plan and Beyond*, Washington DC, Brookings Institution.

**Bartley M** (1993), 'Editorial', *Critical Public Health*, Vol. 4, No. 1, pp.3-6.

**Beauchamp T L & Childress J F** (1983), *Principles of Biomedical Ethics*, (2nd edition), New York, Oxford University Press.

**Benton S** (1994), *Rights to Health and Health Care*, London, IPPR.

**Bleichrodt H** (1993), *Testing the value of expected utility theory in health state evaluation: some experimental results*, Rotterdam, Erasmus University Institute for Medical Technology Assessment.

**Bogdanor V** (1992), 'Neighbourhood watchdog for Whitehall', *The Guardian*, 25 July, p.23.

**Bottomley V** (1993), *Priority Setting in the NHS*, Speech to BMA, King's Fund and Patients' Association Conference, 11 March.

**Bowling A, Jacobson B & Southgate L** (1993), 'Exploration in consultation of the public and health professionals on priority setting in an inner London health district', *Social Science and Medicine*, Vol. 37, No. 7, pp.851-7.

**Boyd K M** (Ed.) (1979), *The Ethics of Resource Allocation in Health Care*, Edinburgh, University of Edinburgh Press.

**Boyne G A** (1992), 'Local government structure and performance: lessons from America?', *Public Administration*, Vol. 70, No. 3, pp.333-58.

**Brannigan M** (1993), 'Oregon's experiment', *Health Care Analysis*, Vol. 1, No. 1, pp.15-32.

**British Medical Association** (1980), *The Handbook of Medical Ethics*, London.

**Calabresi G & Bobbitt P** (1978), *Tragic Choices*, New York, Norton.

**Calnan M, Cant S & Gabe J** (1993), *Going Private: Why People Pay for Their Health Care*, Buckingham, Open University Press.

**Carr-Hill R A** (1991), 'Allocating Resources to Health Care: Is the QALY a Technical Solution to a Potential Problem?', *International Journal of Health Services*, 21, No. 2, pp.351-363.

**Clarke M, Chesworth J & Harrison S** (1993), *Information and National Health Service Purchasing Authorities: the HIPPS System*, Leeds, University of Leeds Nuffield Institute for Health.

**Cochrane A L** (1972), *Effectiveness and Efficiency: Random Reflections on Health Services*, London, Nuffield Provincial Hospitals Trust.

**Coles J** (1993), 'No doctors' dilemma if your health goes up in smoke', *The Guardian*, 22 October, p.23.

**Committee on Social Insurance and Allied Services** (1942), *Report*, Cm. 6404, London, HMSO.

**Coote A** (Ed) (1992) *The Welfare of Citizens: Developing new social rights*, London IPPR/Rivers Oram Press.

**Coote A** (1993), 'Public participation in decisions about health care', *Critical Public Health*, Vol. 4, No. 1, pp.36-48.

**Coote A** (1993), 'The case for social rights', Paper presented at ESRC local governance seminar, Birmingham, 2-4 December.

**Coote A** (Forthcoming) 'Deciding about rights' in Miliband, D *Reinventing the Left*, London, Polity.

**Culyer A J** (1992), 'The morality of efficiency in health care - some uncomfortable implications', *Health Economics*, Vol. 1, No. 1, pp.7-18.

**Culyer A J, Donaldson C & Gerard K** (1988), *Alternatives for Funding Health Services in the U.K.*, London, Institute of Health Services Management.

**Davies P** (1991), 'Thumbs down for Oregon rations', *Health Service Journal*, 14 November, pp.10-11.

**Davies P** (1993), 'Damned if they do, damned if they don't', *Health Service Journal*, 27 May 1993, p.14.

**Department of Health** (1991), *The Patient's Charter*, London.

**Department of Health** (1992), *The Health of the Nation: A Strategy for Health in England*, Cm. 1986, London, HMSO.

**Department of Health and Social Security** (1970), *The Future Structure of the National Health Service*, (The Crossman Green Paper), London, HMSO.

**Department of Health and Social Security** (1972a), *National Health Service Reorganisation: England*, Cmnd. 5055, London, HMSO.

**Department of Health and Social Security** (1972b), *Management Arrangements for the Reorganised National Health Service*, London, HMSO.

**Department of Health and Social Security** (1976), *Priorities for the Health and Personal Social Services in England*, London, HMSO.

**Department of Health and Social Security and Welsh Office** (1979), *Patients First: Consultative Paper on the Structure and Management of the National Health Service in England and Wales*, London, HMSO.

**Dimond B** (1993), 'Decisions, decisions', *Health Service Journal*, 28 January, pp.26-7.

**Dixon J & Welch H G** (1991), 'Priority Setting: Lessons from Oregon', *The Lancet*, Vol. 337, April 13, pp.891-4.

**Doyal L** (1993), 'The role of the public in health care rationing', *Critical Public Health*, Vol. 4, No. 1, pp.49-54.

**Doyal L & Gough I** (1991), *A Theory of Human Need*, Basingstoke, Macmillan.

**Drummond M F & Maynard A K** (eds) (1993), *Purchasing and Providing Cost-Effective Health Care*, Edinburgh, Churchill Livingstone.

**Drummond M, Torrance G & Mason J** (1993), 'Cost-effectiveness league tables: more harm than good?', *Social Science and Medicine*, Vol. 37, No. 1, pp.33-40.

**Dunleavy P & O'Leary B** (1987), *Theories of the State: The Politics of Liberal Democracy*, London, Macmillan.

**Dworkin R** (1994), 'Will Clinton's Plan be Fair?', *New York Review of Books*, 13 January, pp.20-5.

**Eminson J** (1991), 'Why small is beautiful', *Health Service Journal*, 22 August, p.8.

**Eskin F & Bull A R** (1991), 'Squaring a difficult circle', *Health Service Journal*, 10 January, pp.16-8.

**European Group for Health Measurement and Quality of Life Assessment** (1991), 'Cross-cultural adaptation of health measures', *Health Policy*, Vol. 19, No. 1, pp.33-42.

**Evandrou M, Falkingham J, Le Grand J & Winter D** (1992), 'Equity in health and social care', *Journal of Social Policy*, Vol. 21, No. 4, pp.489-523.

**Evans R G** (1990), 'The dog in the night-time: Medical Practice variations and health policy' in T F Andersen and G Mooney (Eds), *The Challenge of Medical Practice Variations*, Basingstoke, Macmillan.

**Ferguson J H, Dubinsky M & Kirsch P J** (1993), 'Court-ordered reimbursement for unproven medical technology: circumventing technology assessment', *Journal of the American Medical Association*, Vol. 269, No. 16, pp.2116-20.

**Fishkin J S** (1979), *Tyranny and Legitimacy: a Critique of Political Theories*, Baltimore, MD, Johns Hopkins University Press.

**Freemantle N** (1993), 'Rationing infertility services', *The Lancet*, Vol. 342, pp.251-2.

**Freemantle N & Harrison S** (1993), 'Interleukin 2: the public and professional face of rationing in the NHS', *Critical Social Policy*, Vol. 13, No. 3, pp.94-117.

**Freemantle N, Long A F, Mason J, Sheldon T A, Song F, Watson P & Wilson C** (1993a), *The Treatment of Depression in Primary Care: Effective Health Care No. 5*, Leeds, University of Leeds School of Public Health and University of York Centre for Health Economics.

**Freemantle N, Long A F, Mason J, Sheldon T A, Song F, Watson P & Wilson C** (1993b), *Cholesterol Screening and Treatment, Effective Health Care No. 6*, Leeds, University of Leeds Nuffield Institute for Health and University of York Centre for Health Economics.

**Fuchs V R** (1974), *Who shall live? Health, economics and social choice*, New York, Basic Books.

**Gafni A & Birch S** (1991), 'Equity considerations in utility-based measures of health outcomes in economic appraisals: an adjustment algorithm', *Journal of Health Economics*, Vol. 10, pp.329-42.

**Gerard K & Mooney G** (1993), 'QALY league tables: handle with care', *Health Economics*, Vol. 2, pp.59-64.

**Giles S** (1993), 'Rationing Scheme will exclude minor illnesses from NHS', *Health Service Journal*, 26 August 1993, p.7.

**Giovannucci E, Ascherio A, Rimm E B, Colditz G A, Stampfer M J, & Willett W C** (1993), A prospective cohort study of vasectomy and prostrate cancer in US men, *Journal of the American Medical Association*, Vol. 269, No. 7, pp.873-7.

**Goldacre M J, Lee A & Don B** (1987), 'Waiting list statistics: relation between admissions from waiting list and length of waiting list', *British Medical Journal*, Vol. 295, pp.1105-8.

**Goodin R E & Wilenski P** (1984), 'Beyond Efficiency: the Logical Underpinnings of Administrative Principles', *Public Administration Review*, Vol. 6, pp.512-517.

**Goodwin B** (1992a), *Justice by Lottery*, Brighton, Harvester.

**Goodwin B** (1992b), *Using Political Ideas*, 3rd edition, Chichester, John Wiley.

**Government Committee on Choices in Health Care** (1992), *Choices in Health Care*, Rijswijk, The Netherlands.

**Gower Davies J** (1972), *The Evangelistic Bureaucrat*, London, Tavistock.

**Griffith S & McMahon L** (1992), *Health Abacus*, London, South-West Thames Regional Health Authority and Office of Public Management.

**Grimes D** (1987), 'Rationing health care', *The Lancet*, 14 March, pp.615-6.

**Gudex C** (1986), *QALYs and Their Use by the Health Service*, Discussion Paper no. 20, York, University of York Centre for Health Economics.

**Haleem M A S A** (1993), 'Medical Ethics in Islam' in A. Grubb (ed), *Choices and Decisions in Health Care*, Chichester, Wiley.

**Ham C** (1985), *The Governance of Health Services*, Community Services Topic Paper No. 1.8, Birmingham, University of Birmingham Department of Social Administration.

**Ham C** (1993), 'Priority Setting in the NHS: reports from six districts', *British Medical Journal*, Vol. 307, pp.435-8.

**Hann A** (1993), *The Politics of Breast Cancer Screening*, Paper presented at the Political Studies Association Conference, Leicester, 20 April.

**Harris E A** (1993), 'Open letter to market-led Ministers of Health', *Healthcare Analysis*, Vol. 1, pp.29-31.

**Harrison S** (1988), *Managing the National Health Service: Shifting the Frontier?*, London, Chapman and Hall.

**Harrison S** (1991), 'Working the markets: purchaser/provider separation in English health care', *International Journal of Health Services*, Vol. 21, No. 4, pp.625-35.

**Harrison S** (1992), 'The Reorganisation After Next? Organising for Health in the UK' in L H W Paine (ed), *British Hospital Management*, pp.25-7, London, Sterling Publications.

**Harrison S, Hunter, D J, Johnston I H, Nicholson N, Thunhurst C & Wistow G** (1991), *Health Before Health Care, Social Policy Paper No. 4*, London, Institute for Public Policy Research.

**Harrison S, Hunter D J & Pollitt C J** (1990), *The Dynamics of British Health Policy*, London, Unwin Hyman.

**Harrison S, Pohlman C E & Mercer G** (1984), *Concepts of Clinical Freedom Amongst English Physicians*, Paper presented at EAPHSS Conference on Clinical Autonomy, King's Fund Centre, 8 June.

**Harrison S & Pollitt C J** (1994), *Controlling Health Professionals*, Buckingham, Open University Press.

**Harrison S & Wistow G** (1992), 'The purchaser/provider split in English health care: towards explicit rationing?', *Policy and Politics*, Vol. 20, No. 2.

***Health Service Journal*** (1993), 'Managers Ponder the Shape of Things to Come', 17 June, pp.12-16.

**Heginbotham C** (1992), 'Rationing', *British Medical Journal*, Vol. 304, pp.496-9.

**Hewitson P, Smith I, Eskin F & Watson P** (1992), *Purchasing for Health Gain: Yorkshire Health Care Cube*, Harrogate, Yorkshire Regional Health Authority.

**Higgins J & Ruddle S** (1991), 'Waiting for a better alternative', *Health Service Journal*, 11 July, pp.18-9.

**Hoffenberg R** (1987), *Clinical Freedom*, London, Nuffield Provincial Hospitals Trust.

**Hoffenberg R** (1992), Letter to the editor, *British Medical Journal*, Vol. 304, p.182.

**Hunt P B** (1993), 'Still open to question', *Health Service Journal*, 16 December, p.21.

**Hunter D J** (1993a), *Rationing Dilemmas in Health Care*, Birmingham, National Association of Health Authorities and Trusts.

**Hunter D J** (1993b), 'Rationing and health gain', *Critical Public Health*, Vol. 4, No. 1, pp.27-32.

**Jennings K** (1993), 'Rationing and older people', *Critical Public Health*, Vol. 4, No. 1, pp.33-5.

**Jonsen A R** (1992), 'Fear of rationing', *Health Management Quarterly*, Vol. XIV, No. 2, pp.6-9.

**Judge K & Solomon M** (1993), 'Public opinion and the National Health Service: patterns and perspectives in consumer satisfaction', *Journal of Social Policy*, Vol. 22, No. 3, pp.299-327.

**Kennedy I** (1993), 'Medicine in Society, Now and in the Future', in S. Lock (ed), *Eighty-five Not Out: Essays in Honour of Sir George Godber*, London, King's Fund.

**Kind P, Rosser R & Williams A** (1982), 'Valuation of Quality of Life: Some Psychometric Evidence' in M W Jones-Lee (Ed), *The Value of Life and Safety*, New York, North Holland.

**Kitzhaber J A** (1993), 'Prioritising Health Services in an Era of Limits: the Oregon Experience', *British Medical Journal*, Vol. 307, pp.373-7.

**Klein R E** (1974), 'The Case for Elitism: Public Opinion and Public Policy', *Political Quarterly*, Vol. 45, No. 4, pp.406-417.

**Klein R E** (1989), *The Politics of the National Health Service*, 2nd edition, London, Longman.

**Klein R E** (1992a), 'Dilemmas and decisions', *Health Management Quarterly*, Vol. XIV, No. 2, pp.2-5.

**Klein R E** (1992b), 'Warning Signals from Oregon', *British Medical Journal*, Vol. 304, pp.1457-8.

**Klein R E** (1993), 'Dimensions of rationing: who should do what?', *British Medical Journal*, Vol. 307, pp.309-11.

**Körner S** (1971), *Fundamental Questions of Philosophy: One Philosopher's Answers*, Brighton, Harvester.

**Labour Party** (1994), *Health 2000: the Health and Wealth of the Nation in the 21st Century*, London.

**Light D W** (1991), 'Effectiveness and efficiency under competition: the Cochrane test', *British Medical Journal*, Vol. 303, pp.1253-4.

**Lindblom C E** (1979), 'Still Muddling, Not Yet Through', *Public Administration Review*, Vol. 39, No. 6, pp.517-526.

**Loughlin M** (1993), 'A reply to Spicker', *Health Care Analysis*, Vol. 1, No. 1, pp.17-20.

**Le Grand J** (1982), *The Strategy of Equality: Redistribution and the Social Services*, London, Allen + Unwin.

**Lukes S** (1973), *Individualism*, Oxford, Blackwell.

**Lyall J** (1993a), 'Doctors' Dilemma?', *Health Services Management*, February, p.25.

**Lyall J** (1993b), 'Trust me, I'm a doctor', *Health Service Journal*, 18 November, p.13.

**Macintyre S, Maciver S & Sooman S** (1993), 'Area, class and health: should we be focusing on places or people?', *Journal of Social Policy*, Vol. 22, Part 2, pp.213-34.

**Magell J** (1985), 'Running Off the Rails', *Hospital Doctor*, 24 October.

**Martin G, Tremblay M & Fletcher S** (1993), Making Choices: a Report on Purchasing Configuration to the Metropolitan Borough of Bolton and the Metropolitan Borough of Wigan, Birmingham, University of Birmingham Health Services Management Centre.

**Maynard A K** (1993), 'Future directions for health-care reform' in M.F. Drummond and A.K. Maynard (eds), *Purchasing and Providing Cost-Effective Health Care*, Edinburgh, Churchill Livingstone.

**Mays N** (1993), 'What are the effects of integration in the N.I. health and personal social services?', *Critical Public Health*, Vol. 4, No. 2, pp.43-8.

**McGuire A** (1986), 'Ethics and resource allocation: an economist's view', *Social Science and Medicine*, Vol. 22, No. 11, pp.1167-74.

**McGuire A, Henderson J & Mooney G** (1988), *The Economics of Health Care: An Introductory Text*, London, Routledge and Kegan Paul.

**McHale J & Hughes D** (1993), 'Down by law', *Health Service Journal*, 26 August, p.33.

**Meek C** (1992), 'Pie in the sky: can health care rationing ever be objective?', *BMA News Review*, September, pp.15-7.

**Ministry of Health and Department of Health for Scotland** (1944), *A National Health Service*, Cmnd 6502, London, HMSO.

**Mooney G, Gerard K, Donaldson C & Farrar S** (1992), *Priority Setting in Purchasing: Some Practical Guidelines*, Birmingham, National Association of Health Authorities and Trusts.

**Mooney G H, Russell E M & Weir R D** (1980), *Choices for Health Care*, London, Macmillan.

**Mulkay M, Ashmore M & Pinch T** (1987), 'Measuring the Quality of Life: A Sociological Invention Concerning the Application of Economics to Health Care', *Sociology*, Vol. 21, No. 4, pp.541-564.

**National Association of Health Authorities and Trusts** (1993), *Securing Effective Public Accountability in the NHS: A Discussion Paper*, Birmingham.

**NHS Management Executive** (1993), *League Tables of Performance*, EL(93)64, Leeds, NHSME.

**OECD** (1987), *Financing and Delivering Health Care*, Paris, Organisation for Economic Co-operation and Development.

**Parker R** (1975), 'Social administration and scarcity' in E Butterworth and R Holtman (Eds), *Social Welfare in Modern Britain*, pp.204-12, London, Fontana.

**Parsonage M & Neuberger H** (1992), 'Discounting and Health Benefits', *Health Economics*, Vol. 1, pp.71-9.

**Paton C R** (1993), *National Health Policy: Issues, Options and Choices*, Paper presented to Institute of Public Policy Research Seminar, 27 April.

**Petrou S & Renton A** (1993), 'The QALY: a guide for the public health physician', *Public Health*, Vol. 107, pp.327-36.

**Piachaud D & Weddell J M** (1972), 'The Economics of Treating Varicose Veins', *International Journal of Epidemiology*, Vol. 1, No. 3, pp.287-294.

**Pollock A** (1993), 'Rationing - implicit, explicit, or merely complicit?', *Critical Public Health*, Vol. 4, No. 1, pp.19-22.

**Rawls J** (1971), *A Theory of Justice*, Oxford, Oxford University Press.

**Redmayne S & Klein R E** (1993), 'Rationing in practice: the case of *in vitro* fertilisation', *British Medical Journal*, Vol. 306, pp.1521-4.

**Redmayne S, Klein R E & Day P** (1993), *Sharing Out Resources: Purchasing and Priority Setting in the NHS*, Birmingham, National Association of Health Authorities and Trusts.

**Regan D E & Stewart J** (1982), 'An essay in the local government of health: the case for local authority control', *Social Policy and Administration*, Vol. 16, No. 1, pp.19-43.

**Resource Allocation Working Party** (1976), *Sharing Resources for Health in England*, London, HMSO.

**Roberts F** (1952), *The Cost of Health*, London, Turnstile Press.

**Salter B** (1992), *The Politics of Purchasing in the NHS*, Canterbury, University of Kent at Canterbury Centre for Health Services Studies.

**Salter B** (1993), 'The politics of purchasing in the National Health Service', *Policy and Politics*, Vol. 21, No. 3, pp.171-84.

**Sheldon T A & Carr-Hill R** (1992), 'Resource allocation by regression in the National Health Service: a critique of the Resource Allocation Working Party's review', *Journal of the Royal Statistical Society*, Vol. 155, pp.403-20.

**Shiu M** (1993), 'Refusing to treat smokers is unethical and a dangerous precedent', *British Medical Journal*, Vol. 306, pp.1048-9.

**Smith I J** (1992), 'Ethics and health care rationing - new challenges for the public sector manager', *Journal of Management in Medicine*, Vol. 6, No. 1, pp.54-61.

**Spicker S F** (1993), 'Going off the dole: a prudential and ethical critique of the healthfare state', *Health Care Analysis*, Vol. 1, No. 1, pp.11-16.

**Stewart J** (1990), 'Local government: new thinking on neglected issues', *Public Money and Management*, Vol. 10, No. 2, pp.59-60.

**Stewart J D** (1992), *Accountability to the Public*, London, European Policy Forum.

**Stewart J D** (forthcoming) *Citizens' Juries*, London, IPPR.
Taylor-Gooby P. (1985), 'Attitudes to Welfare', *Journal of Social Policy*, Vol. 14, Pt. 1, pp.73-81.

**Thain C & Wright M** (1991), 'Trends in Public Expenditure', *B887: Managing Public Services*, Unit 3, Milton Keynes, Open University.

**Titmuss R M** (1973), *The Gift Relationship*, Harmondsworth, Penguin Books.

**Tomlin Z** (1992), 'Their treatment in your hands', *The Guardian*, 24 April, p.21.

**Torrance G W** (1984), *Health Status Measurement for Economic Appraisal*, Paper presented at Health Economists' Study Group Meeting, Aberdeen, 3-4 July.

**Townsend P & Davidson N** (Eds) (1983), *Inequalities in Health: the Black Report*, Harmondsworth, Penguin Books.

**Tremblay M** (1993), Letter to the Editor, *Health Service Journal*, 25 November, p.20.

**Ubel P A, Arnold R M & Caplan A L** (1993), 'Rationing failure: the ethical lessons of the re-transplantation of scarce vital organs', *Journal of the American Medical Association*, Vol. 270, no. 20, pp.2469-74.

**van Williganburg T** (1993), 'Communitarian Illusions: or why the Dutch proposal for setting priorities in health care must fail', *Health Care Analysis*, Vol. 1, No. 1, pp.49-52.

**Wandsworth Borough Council** (1993), *Report to Special Policy and Finance Committee, 10 November: Current Issues Relating to the National Health Service locally that affect the Borough*, London.

**Watkin B** (1978), The National Health Service: The First Phase - 1948-1974 and After, London, Allen and Unwin.

**Weale A** (1983), *Political Theory and Social Policy*, London, Macmillan.

**Wennberg J** (1990), 'Outcomes research cost containment, and the fear of health care rationing', *New England Journal of Medicine*, Vol. 323, pp.1202-4.

**Whitehead M** (1992), 'The concepts and principles of equity and health', *International Journal of Health Services*, Vol. 22, No. 3, pp.429-55.

**Williams A H** (1985), *Medical Ethics: Health Service Efficiency and Clinical Freedom*, Nuffield/York Portfolio No. 2, London, Nuffield Provincial Hospitals Trust.

**Williams M & Frankel S** (1993), 'The myth of infinite demand', *Critical Public Health*, Vol. 4, No. 1, pp.13-18.

**Wistow G** (1993), 'Democratic Deficit', *Community Care*, 30 September, p.29.

**World Bank** (1993), *World Development Report 1993: Investing in Health*, New York, Oxford University Press.

**Zwart H** (1993), 'Rationale in the Netherlands: the Liberal and Communitarian Perspective', *Health Care Analysis*, Vol. 1, No. 1, pp.53-6.

## Some IPPR Publications:

*Understanding Local Needs*
**Janie Percy-Smith & Ian Sanderson**
**Dec 1992 ISBN 1 872452 59 0 £9.95**

Reports on a pilot 'needs audit' which suggests a model for involving citizens in defining welfare needs.

*The Welfare of Citizens: Developing New Social Rights*
**Edited by Anna Coote**
**June 1992 ISBN 1 854890 38 7 £9.95**

Argues that citizenship in a modern democracy must embody social and economic as well as civil and political rights. Papers by Raymond Plant, Norman Lewis, Wendy Thomson and others include proposals for a charter of social rights; rules for procedural fairness; a role for locally negotiated service contracts and a new approach to the development of children's rights.

*Is Quality Good for You? A Critical Review of Quality Assurance in Welfare Services*
**Naomi Pfeffer & Anna Coote**
**July 1991 ISBN 1 872452 36 1 £10**

Explores the politics behind the pursuit of quality in public services. Proposes a new 'democratic' approach for a modern welfare system seeking to reconcile equity and freedom.

'an excellent introduction to the current debates'.
*Critical Public Health*

*Child Care in a Modern Welfare System: Towards a New National Policy*
**Bronwen Cohen & Neil Fraser**
**Aug 1991   ISBN 1 872452 41 8   £10**

Child care should play an important role in a modern welfare system. Practical proposals for flexible and responsive child care services.

'it sets out the basis for the kind of coherent national policy so desperately needed.'
*Times Educational Supplement*

*Equal Rights for Disabled People: The Case for a New Law*
**Ian Bynoe, Mike Oliver & Colin Barnes**
**Sept 1991   ISBN 1 872452 43 4   £5**

Proposals for a law against unfair discrimination on grounds of disability.

*The Family Way:  A New Approach to Policy-Making*
**Anna Coote, Harriet Harman & Patricia Hewitt**
**Sept 1990   ISBN 1 872452 15 9   £10**

The most comprehensive analysis of changing patterns of family life and their implications for policy.

'The Government should swallow its pride and adopt this proposal'.
*Sunday Mirror*

*Health before Health Care*
**Stephen Harrison *et al***
**June 1991   ISBN 1 872452 34 5   £3**